Christ, Crime, and Moral Judgment

Christ, Crime, and Moral Judgment

CHARLES P. NEMETH

ST. AUGUSTINE'S PRESS

South Bend, Indiana

Manufactured in the United States of America.

1 2 3 4 5 6 30 29 28 27 26 25

Library of Congress Control Number: 2025932178

Paperback ISBN: 978-1-58731-119-2
Ebook ISBN: 978-1-58731-120-8

∞ The paper used in this publication meets the minimum requirements of the American National Standard for Information Sciences – Permanence of Paper for Printed Materials, ANSI Z39.48-1984.

St. Augustine's Press
www.staugustine.net

To my grandchildren, whose lives lie ahead and who each will make a positive and special difference.

To: *Theresa, Rachel, Charlotte, Cecilia, McKenna, Savannah, William Charles, Charles Joseph, Maive Lily*

To: St. Thomas Aquinas who stated:

> If the judge knows that a man who has been convicted by false witnesses is innocent, he must, like Daniel, examine the witnesses with great care, so as to find a motive for acquitting the innocent: but if he cannot do this he should remit him for judgment by a higher tribunal. If even this is impossible, he does not sin if he pronounce sentence in accordance with the evidence, for it is not he that puts the innocent man to death, but they who stated him to be guilty. He that carries out the sentence of the judge who has condemned an innocent man, if the sentence contains an inexcusable error, he should not obey.

Thomas Aquinas, *Summa Theologiae*, II-II, q. 64, a. 6, ad. 2 in Summa Theologica: Complete English Edition in Five Volumes, trans. Fathers of the English Dominican Province (Christian Classics, 1981), https://www.newadvent.org/summa/3064.htm.

Table of Contents

Preface

Christ, Crime, and Moral Judgment is a work of first instance that creates a compendium of designated crimes explicitly referenced by Jesus Christ. After nearly four decades involved in criminal law and its practice, I had hoped to discern the root origins of contemporary criminal law by visiting the perpetual and perfect wisdom of Jesus Christ. While not all crimes are covered, the reader will be impressed by the depth and breadth of Christ's coverage of crime. It will not take long to see the intersection of the law of crimes and the perfect philosophy of Christ.

Chapter 1's stress is to deal with first principles when it comes to the idea of moral judgment. Too many caricatures and stereotypes of Jesus tend to paint Him as soft on error and crime and tolerant without limits. Indeed, a host of forces have propped up the Jesus of non-judgment and His capacity to forgive without any reference to repentance and change. Christ's philosophy is far more complex. Added to this, the chapter reminds readers of the forces that have shaped this excessive tolerance, especially from the schools of libertarianism, liberalism, and the incorrect theological teaching that have been on the rise.

In Chapter 2, the reader encounters the definition and method of moral judgment. While various critics of moral judgment, especially the moral relativist and those who deny the existence of any objective moral truth, claim moral judgment is not possible or too impositional, the Coming of Jesus Christ is grounded in the essence of moral judgment. His very Incarnation presumes the need for moral judgment. The second major aspect of the chapter is how moral judgment is a rational exercise dependent on some level of certitude in human action. How the intellect deliberates, counsels, and chooses shows the method of making wise moral judgments. Lastly, the chapter uses Hell as proof of the need and requirement for moral judgment. Otherwise, the afterlife would lose all meaning.

Chapter 3 concentrates on the heritage and legacy evident in Christian tradition and how the Decalogue resides at the center of the crimes code soon to unfold in the book. In more general terms, it is Christ who has been prophesied to come into the world to save it. The chapter provides text and language which foretells the Messiah's coming long before its historical occurrence. Then, more specifically, the chapter looks at the express language and delineation discoverable in the Decalogue as to specific crimes. The chapter correlates the Ten Commandments to specific contemporary criminal behavior. After this the stress is on the actual language of Jesus Christ, who frequently references the Decalogue but also reiterates prohibited felonious conduct. A failure to adhere to the Commandments and His proscriptions will result in a loss of eternal life.

Chapters 4 ventures into specific crimes, such as murder and assault, as well as other offenses against the body. In the matter of murder, Christ lays out its two-tier requirement—the proof of act and the proof of a culpable mind. In modern terms, this is known as Actus Reus and Mens Rea, respectively. Christ comments that the murder must come from within—from inside the mind and heart of the criminal actor. As Christ does with most offenses, He makes repeated references to the Decalogue, which expressly forbids unjustified murder and killing. Quite provocatively, He also references how religious leaders commit murder in the name of religion—a subtle reference to John the Baptist. The remainder of the chapter deals with assault in its various forms. At the same time, Jesus urges His followers to seek peace and to avoid confrontation in minor bodily cases. Otherwise, the smaller offense evolves into larger criminality and strife.

Chapter 5 deals with sexual offenses. While not a precise categorization of sexual crimes, the commentary stresses the role of vices, particularly lust, in the conclusion that behavior is improper. While Christ never directly defines rape, His assessment of lewd, lascivious, and debaucherous behavior closely ties to the aggressive growth of sexual error and harm. His analysis of adultery paints a picture not anticipated by modern thinking, for Christ concludes that the act of adultery always leads to other sexual impropriety. Even lust in one's mind, coveting a neighbor's wife in thought alone, equates with the actual commission. Finally, Jesus reserves special judgments for those who abuse and harm children, and His harsh assessment manifests the almost satanic quality of these harms.

In Chapter 6, the reader is introduced to Christ's comprehensive coverage of property crime. The extent of property crime depends, to some extent, on the nature of the economic system in place. Various commentators argue that Jesus tends toward collective ownership, though this view is simplistic and disregards the balance Jesus exhorts His followers to achieve in the matter of property. Having too much or too little is not a place Jesus seems to prefer and, in its place, find the mean between having sufficient property to live decently although excessive materialism is frowned upon. Starting with the Decalogue, both the Eighth and Tenth Commandments provide a rationale for the condemnation of theft, extortion, fraud, robbery, and deceit. The chapter also edifies the sophisticated perspective of how positions of authority, from soldier to temple priest, are utilized to justify property crimes. Highlighted will be the extreme facts of Jesus clearing the Temple from the "den of robbers."

Chapter 7 ends the examination by laying out Christ's plan for salvation and redemption for even hardened criminals. For most criminal perpetrators, the rehabilitative plan has little if any chance of success, if relying upon the secular system of correctional reform. In Christ, there is a hopeful remediation, but it will depend on the criminal agent achieving three distinct steps: repent, seek forgiveness, and change.

Acknowledgments

After authoring so many works on law and justice, jurisprudence and legal philosophy, I am certain that much of what I have produced over the years depended upon others. Nothing is done in isolation, and in fact, I am utterly humbled by those whose talents and skills make these projects a reality. And I realize that publishers get nervous about projects like this and take a safer road at the expense of seeing Christ from the angle espoused in this work. For that I am thankful to St. Augustine's Press for being the publisher. In particular, I offer thanks to its Publisher in Chief, Benjamin Fingerhut, and the Editor Catherine Godfrey.

On the production end, I thankfully continue my long and very fruitful association with Hope Haywood whose penchant for orderliness and precision is quite special and even unrivaled. Hope has been with me for a long journey. Never a day passes when I do not value her extraordinary talents.

On this project, I was also fully blessed to have a student researcher whose skill and keenness of mind got me moving in all the directions possible. Theresa Ryan, a Franciscan student, who double majors in Theology and Criminal Justice, performed at levels not often witnessed in an undergraduate. Theresa's passion for the project and the subject matter is what vivifies so much of this research. I am deeply grateful.

At Franciscan University of Steubenville, I labor in an environment that spurs on projects of this genre. Since my retirement from John Jay College, I never envisioned I would work in an environment so encouraging and so passionate about the Catholic faith. Here faith is lived out in every corner of the campus. It was only a matter of time before I would conceive this book, for the culture and ethos of Franciscan gets you thinking about these sorts of topics. Under the leadership of President Father Dave Pivonka and the VPAA Dr. Stephen Hildebrand, faculty are encouraged to integrate their Catholic faith into every inch of what the faculty member can tackle. Finally, I am fortunate to work in the School of Professional Programs, whose Dean, Dr. Chrissy Jungers, fosters an environment of collegiality and creativity. Dr. Jungers is always there to support you along the way.

Finally, my spouse and closest friend of fifty-three years, Jean Marie, is forever the sounding board on ideas I have posed over the years. Her record on predictions as to success in particular works has been near perfect, and on this project, there was not a scintilla or reservation.

Charles P. Nemeth, JD, PhD, LL.M
Professor and Director of Criminal Justice
Director of the Center of Criminal Justice, Law, and Ethics
Franciscan University of Steubenville
Steubenville, OH

Chapter 1: Moral Judgment in Christian Tradition: Christ, Crime, and Moral Judgment

Introduction: The Idea and Definition of Moral Judgment

People judge things all the time. One can judge the weather, or one can judge the quality or lack thereof in the taste of food, furniture, a sunset at the beach, and the beauty of a winter storm. Most of us engage in daily judgments by making decisions about how we carry out human life. Few people fret over these sorts of pedantic conclusions, for most of our decision-making lacks a moral feel or dimension. In matters of morals, the issue of moral judgment seems to cause the most consternation. Some would argue that choices in moral matters are far too qualitative rather than quantitative—that a science of moral judgment may be illusive. On the other hand, moral determinations are crucial, even utterly essential, to any civilization. A culture, a country, and a nation-state that lacks morality, or even one with a bad, errant morality, is bound to fail. History is replete with examples of this.

The idea of moral judgment has woven its way through all civilized time. In general, moral judgment connotes a decision about choice in moral matters.[1]

One recent commentator sought to relegate the subject matter of morality to making choices between one conduct or another. Moral judgment "uses the distinction between moral standards and responsibility standards to clarify the difference between praise and

1

condemnation, which are related to the former, and blame and credit, which are related to the latter. It shows that the phrases, morally good, morally bad, morally right, morally wrong, and morally ought are not redundant, and differ in meaning from good, bad, right, wrong, and ought."[2]

By what criteria one makes moral judgments greatly varies. Pope Benedict will argue that moral determinations depend on fixed, objective truth rooted in the natural law, a continuation of the long influence of Thomism in the Church's moral philosophy. Benedict's view is labeled "normative morality."[3] For those without an objective measure of any sort, one wonders whether any dependable moral philosophy can ever be developed, and even more so, depended upon. From a host of other contexts, we find concerted efforts to simply do away with all sense of personal responsibility, to avoid culpability or moral accountability for just about every sort of human action. James Q. Wilson's splendid analysis on moral judgment, or the lack thereof in the justice system, labels it a crisis of the "abuse excuse." In our current justice model, the idea of personal responsibility and accountability has all but vanished.[4] As our justice model and our cultural tolerance levels continue down this path, one soon discovers that even the Supreme Judge of human behavior, namely Jesus Christ, despite His perfect and unassailable sense of justice and moral judgment, moral determination and choice, fits uncomfortably in a world that avoids judgment. See Figure 1 on the next page.

In the matter of moral and ethical judgment, the Son of God, Jesus Christ, has been recast into an unrecognizable caricature. Modern thinking tends to type Jesus as a "happy-slappy" figure whose reservoir for forgiveness is simply boundless. Jesus never judges, nor does Jesus really ever condemn according to many contemporaries. Reliant upon selected Scriptures, those who favor the non-judgmental Jesus perpetually cite the verse "Do not judge, so that you may not be judged."[5]

2

The power of this admonition is quite attractive in the circles of those who wish to withhold judgment on human action, and it is especially appealing to a whole strand of thinkers who would rather not judge but just mind one's own business. Then too, other thinkers will avoid judgment except in cases of selective outrage— something utterly evident in the gulags of political correctness and modern liberalism. And maybe the term liberalism has long been vanquished by the newer forms of irrationality that border on a fascistic irrationality. This fringe of crushing judgment under the guise of tolerance is witnessed in transgenderism, whether in sports or bathrooms, DEI (diversity, equity, or inclusion) or eternal Affirmative Action. What is patently obvious is that the work of making judgments is now suspect, even an impossibility, in many circles.

Herein is a short review of the more dominant schools that are uneasy with true moral judgment.

Libertarianism and Non-Judgment

Libertarians, by way of illustration, endlessly tout silly maxims like "it is none of my business," or "as long as it does not impact my world," or the even more incredulous "as long as no one is hurt or harmed" I shall withhold judgment. Nathan Schluter's *First Things* critique entitled "Libertarian Delusions" keenly demonstrates how judgment about most issues falters in a libertarian world:

> This means that the state must be neutral with respect to how different individuals understand and pursue what is good (so long as those pursuits do not involve unjust coercion). Such neutrality is attractive because it promises to depoliticize the bitter, exhausting, and seemingly unending culture wars over such matters as pornography, homosexuality, and marriage that have divided Americans.[6]

Remaining neutral on this or that cannot generate a culture that makes moral judgments, but rather a system that avoids making judgments. It is one of the reasons critics of libertarianism see it as a dangerous movement that softens the moral vision and outlook. It is also one of the chief reasons that this movement has no difficulty with so many behaviors, drugs or sexual orientation to name a few. Why make any moral judgment when it falls outside my purview or practice? James Brennan argues that libertarian thought falls into only one school of moral judgment—the "pluralistic" rather than the "monist" view. He explains:

> All moral theories are either monist or pluralist. A monist theory of right action holds that exactly one fundamental feature of actions determines whether they are right and wrong. A pluralist theory holds that more than one fundamental feature determines whether actions are right and wrong. A monist might agree that in commonsense morality, many features seem to count for and against the rightness of actions, but then holds that these features can be reduced to

one deeper or more fundamental feature. The pluralist holds that many features count for or against the rightness of actions, but these features cannot be reduced to one deeper or more fundamental feature.[7]

Hence, the moral theory and moral conceptualization of Jesus Christ is a harder pill to swallow for it is singularly grounded in objective moral truth—it is a hard path to follow and adhere to. Jesus is the Way, the Truth, and the Life for all—not a pluralistic mindset that leads to a vapid isolationism and allows the world to crumble around us.

Modern Liberalism and Judgment

It was not long ago that classical liberalism was capable of reaching moral conclusions on select behavior. Both liberals and conservatives alike could reach similar conclusions on a host of topics once universally frowned upon. Even up until the mid-twentieth century a moral consensus was identifiable on matters of marriage, death and life, suicide and euthanasia, abortion at late term, sexual orientation, and even trivial matters in the so-called advanced state of civilization we find ourselves in like promiscuity, fornication, and adultery. These latter categories are no longer worthy of our consideration in any judgmental context.

In contrast to the libertarian, the liberal is quite content, and even feverishly so, in making judgments about things one may disagree with or not. While the libertarian wants to avoid judgments, the modern liberal-radical has a boatload of judgments that you must agree with or become marginalized or demonized. Political correctness encompasses this phenomenon as does the suffocating world of DEI. These positions and propositions are considered so sacrosanct and self-justifying that disagreement is verboten. Instead, according to the usual protocol of moral evaluation, determining whether something is morally correct or true, advocates for the current crop of liberal leftism will do all in their power to destroy the opposition. Modern liberalism makes judgments constantly and for the most part, very incorrectly. Modern liberalism connotes a tyrannical army of trained and unapologetic zealots, and usually about topics where people of good will and good faith should and must disagree. To illustrate, the modern liberal, although not all admittedly, agree with the exercise of reproductive freedom up to and including the date of birth. That is an irrefutable judgment for many on that side of the pro-choice movement. In this way, judgments are being made. The same could be said about the state of marriage, or the parties to a marriage, or whether drag queens should be reading stories in the children's libraries, or that the Last Supper can be parodied by thirteen drag queens that mock Christianity. These actions are the result of a judgment, and whether any of them are up to any standard of morality is very questionable. Any critique or disagreement with these conclusions is not permitted under the current state of affairs. For to judge otherwise, we are so often told, is a sign of some phobia, some hate or lack of inclusiveness. What we are witnessing in the modern liberal state is not freedom of thought but a tyrannical system of think and thought-speak, where judgment to the opposite is not permissible.

As a result of this suffocating mind control, moral judgments have their life snuffed out without mercy or the so-called tolerance these intolerant groups and advocates so frequently clamor about. At no place is this more obvious than on the modern university or college campus—once havens for Socratic thought and Platonic Academies, they are now havens for terrorist protest, systematic thought control, propaganda, and the radical transformation of reality. Gone are the days of the Great Books and the perennially admired works of the West's greatest minds which are instead being replaced by the whining, grinding, and anguish of victimized groups and classes. Gone are the days when students graduated with a moral vision. This has instead been replaced with a chaotic, indiscernible moral sense governed by fad and trend. Is it any wonder that today's young wallow in self-doubt, commit suicide at alarming rates, are medicated to the point of oblivion and generally operate in complete moral confusion?

The liberal state of affairs has also ushered in a moral and cultural relativity that simply precludes moral reasoning and moral judgment. It is difficult to morally evaluate human affairs as being right or wrong when there is no constancy or objectivity but, instead, a series of personal preferences and individualistic findings that vary from person to person. Both Popes Benedict XVI and John Paul II constantly warned us about being trapped in the circular reasoning so obvious in moral relativity.[8] If something may or may not be true, depending upon circumstances or individual utility, then nothing will ever be true. Relativity overwhelms any chance at reasoned moral judgment. St. John Paul II's magnificent encyclical *Veritatis Splendor* captures the inevitability of a world incapable of making judgments beyond individual wish or preference.

> As is immediately evident, *the crisis of truth* is not unconnected with this development. Once the idea of a universal truth about the good, knowable by human reason, is lost, inevitably the notion of conscience also changes. Conscience is no longer considered in its primordial reality as an act of a person's intelligence, the function of which is to apply the universal knowledge of the good in a specific situation and thus to express a judgment about the right conduct to be chosen here and now. Instead, there is a tendency to grant to the individual conscience the prerogative of independently determining the criteria of good and evil and then acting accordingly. Such an outlook is quite

congenial to an individualist ethic, wherein each individual is faced with his own truth, different from the truth of others. Taken to its extreme consequences, this individualism leads to a denial of the very idea of human nature.[9]

All through the latter part of the twentieth into the twenty-first century, we have encountered the scourge of relativity, whereby marriage and childbirth are really personal choices, or mantras like "love the one you are with," or the even worse "if it feels good, do it." It is also miraculous the culture still stands. Nothing can be judged—not pornography, not adultery, not promiscuity, productive lifestyles, or non-contributing citizenry, nor illegal aliens, or promoters of infanticide. Everything eventually becomes off-limits for the relativist, who in the end is incapable of making a moral judgment.

The Empirical Proof that Moral Judgment Lacks Rationality

New schools continue to emerge in the scholarly community which seeks to eradicate even the possibility of moral judgment due to its flawed empirical proof. One of the more prominent is typed the "Moral Abolitionism Movement." One of its advocates is Hanno Sauer, who recently wrote:

> I argue that recent evidence regarding the psychological basis of moral cognition supports a form of (moderate) moral abolitionism. I identify three main problems undermining the epistemic quality of our moral judgments—contamination, reliability, and bad incentives—and reject three possible responses: neither moral expertise, nor moral learning, nor the possibility

of moral progress succeed in solving the aforementioned epistemic problems. The result is a moderate form of moral abolitionism, according to which we should make fewer moral judgments much more carefully.[10]

Others refer to this sort of approach as "rational pessimism"—a full and final recognition that the aim of the Enlightenment is dead and gone.[11]

Related to this mentality is the absurd conclusion that moral judgment leads to intolerance and a "moral smugness" that should not be allowed. Rather than making judgments, we should avoid them, and in this way, we display a natural tolerance more generous than those who issue moral judgments. Adherents to this school consistently fail to mention their own intolerance of those who make moral judgments. This mentality courses its way through many aspects of modern life—the type of speech we shall permit; the types of beliefs and ideals we wish to adhere to but are frowned upon by those incapable of making any moral judgment except against those who make moral judgments. The "smugness" is on that shoe to be sure.[12]

Even more condescending in this contemporary thread is the accusation that those who hold that moral decline is accelerating suffer from sweeping delusions. In other words, even though the crime data manifests a very negative reality, or that the rate of divorce and negative impacts on the nuclear family have become self-evident, or that substance abuse in the general population is growing at frightful rates, any moral judgments concerning these or any signs of cultural and moral rot are not to be believed. And if they are not to be believed, they cannot and do not exist.[13]

These examples partially represent an environment in which moral judgment has become increasingly unpopular and even unacceptable.

Theological Contortions and Moral Judgment

Aside from cultural, political, and social movements, the problems associated with moral judgments have not been made easier by some theological leaders and their corresponding pronouncements. None illustrates the moral judgment dilemma more than the comments of Pope Francis during the earliest days of his papacy. In response to a question as to how he would act as a confessor to a gay person, his response was "Who am I to judge?"[14]

While the comment appears merciful, and correctly so, it is also dismissive of his role to make judgments as he carries out his confessor role. If he chooses not to do so, the Pope has reached the opposite conclusion, or at least silently so, to issue no judgment. Pope Francis's commentary on this event continues with the publication of his book *The Name of God is Mercy*. He gets more detailed:

> "On that occasion I said this: If a person is gay and seeks out the Lord and is willing, who am I to judge that person?" the pope says. "I was paraphrasing by heart the *Catechism of the Catholic Church* where it says these people should be treated with delicacy and not be marginalized."
>
> "I am glad that we are talking about 'homosexual people' because before all else comes the individual person, in his wholeness and dignity," he continues. "And people should not be defined only by their sexual tendencies: let us not forget that God loves all his creatures and we are destined to receive his infinite love."[15]

No one is denying the propriety and goodness of this statement, yet at the same time, it infers that those that make judgments automatically marginalize and dehumanize others. If this is the standard, we would be hopelessly adrift in matters of moral judgment and tolerate everything and everyone. The pedophile and the saint would be one and the same; the murderer and the child molester immune to judgment. Even Pope Francis appreciates that something more must happen when he holds:

> "I prefer that homosexuals come to confession, that they stay close to the Lord, and that we pray all together," says Francis. "You can advise them to pray, show goodwill, show them the way, and accompany them along it."[16]

If the Pope were not making a judgment, why would he insist on confession and being shown the way? Is this merely a question of method or style rather than the abandonment of judgment?

This is but one case that challenges the more objective norm of judgments that have long been part of Catholic and Christian moral philosophy and theology. There is nothing here that has not been previously considered and reduced to catechetical or pastoral teachings. All of these once irrefutable conclusions are now under siege as well. While the Church has reaffirmed traditional marriage between a man and woman, theological leaders, including Pope Francis, are making waves by softening the judgment. One way this has occurred was the "blessings" of same sex unions—something promoted in various Vatican offices.[17]

While the Vatican played verbal gymnastics with the word "blessings," it was equally obtuse and confusing as to whether this was blessing the unions or just the individuals who are in the union, and the corrosion or moral judgment marches on. As Vatican officials dance on the head of a proverbial pin, the general Church member is left in a sea of indecision and confused messaging. If one can bless, how can I condemn, disagree with, or simply judge this behavior?

The wreckage is emanating from the German Synod on Synodality, which wants to do away with any proscription on sexual orientation and to declare once condemned sexual practices now as normative as the heterosexual practice. Here, as elsewhere in the Church, these once judged practices are being unshackled and recast in a different light. German bishops, by a vote of 18–3, approved the following Motion to bless same sex marriages:

Introduction

The Church wants to unequivocally proclaim the message of the God-given dignity of every person in word and deed. This message guides her in her dealings with people and their partnerships. Therefore, she offers recognition and accompaniment to couples who are united in love, who treat each other with full respect and dignity, and who are prepared to live their sexuality for the long term with care for themselves, for each other and in social responsibility. There are couples who ask for a blessing for their partnership. This request is based on the gratitude for experienced love and the hope for an accompanied future. It is an expression of a relationship with God either of one or of both partners.

Motion

The Synodal Assembly calls on the bishops to officially allow blessing ceremonies in their dioceses for couples who love each other but to whom sacramental marriage is not accessible or who do not see themselves at a point of entering into a sacramental marriage. This also applies to same-sex couples on the basis of a re-evaluation of homosexuality as a norm variant of human sexuality.[18]

To read the words of the Motion is to witness the unraveling of a Church in striking turmoil—a Church that lacks the once vaunted objective consensus. The bishops call for a "re-evaluation of homosexuality as a norm variant for human sexuality." If this be so, the entire moral superstructure and natural law edifice upon which Catholic philosophy and theology rest shall collapse in short order. Even Pope Francis drew the line in the sand and indicated no further. And in this way, he made another judgment by calling out the errant judgment of the eighteen bishops of Germany. Various communications between the Pope and Vatican offices have called out the radical shift from Church teachings. The Pope remarked on November 10, 2023, "There are indeed numerous steps being taken by significant segments of this local Church that threaten to steer it increasingly away from the universal Church's common path."[19]

Again, Pope Francis makes a moral judgment—and curiously, he has been severely critiqued for upholding the objective, catechetical, and moral framework of the Church he leads. It is not always easy to be judgment free or to issue neutral findings that satisfy both sides. Some matters can be defended and some not; some subject to compromise and some not. In this setting resides the world of moral judgment.

At the same time, the teachings of our Savior, Jesus Christ, declare truth in all things and issue moral judgments with dependability and perfection. What will be unfolded in the following pages is precisely how Jesus judges and the manner in which His judgments are always a perfect blend of justice, mercy, compassion, and accountability. And you shall encounter His very exact and precise language when evaluating the propriety of human conduct. What will be most striking is how Jesus is making judgments with extraordinary regularity and clarity on a host of topics.

For most of this work, we shall try to catalog the many places Jesus makes moral judgments. The catalog will largely be a delineation of those behaviors condemned and those that have a common place nomenclature in the law of crimes. Just as the Ten Commandments have long been touted as one of the earliest of criminal codes, so too have the teaching of Jesus Christ, where crimes of every sort are considered and scrutinized. In the end, you shall be neither lost nor confused, and instead, peaceful with how and when to make judgments. Just as critically, you shall see what conduct Jesus negatively judges, but also how to judge—how to temper judgment with mercy, Christian love, and compassion. For Christ, the condemnation is never far from the method—something most moderns tend to favor, that is, the method at the expense of the condemnation. At the beginning of this chapter, we encountered Christ's very famous comment: "Judge not, that you may not be judged."[20] This is but the beginning of a highly complex recitation on that blend of judgment and mercy, for the quote includes additional observations. Jesus never forbids judgment; instead, He urges His followers to go about the business of moral judgment with humility and decency.

> For with what judgment you judge, you shall be judged: and with what measure you mete, it shall be measured to you again. And why seest thou the mote that is in thy brother's eye; and seest not the beam that is in thy own eye? Or how sayest thou to thy brother: Let me cast the mote out of thy eye; and behold a beam is in thy own eye? Thou hypocrite, cast out first the beam in thy own eye, and then shalt thou see to cast out the mote out of thy brother's eye.[21]

What does Jesus mean by the mote and the beam? The "mote" is but a speck of some substance—something small or minor—while the "beam" is the large log or substantial piece of something. In the latter case, Jesus reminds those who heavily judge to remember their own failures first—in this way their judgments are tempered not in terms righteousness or correctness, but in terms of reaction and formal condemnation. Put another way, the judgment of sin and error is perfectly appropriate, although the means and method of said judgment are equally important.

In this way, Jesus blends the law of love and charity with conclusions of justice—a tact that upholds the Law of the Prophets while reminding those who judge to do so in charity.

Conclusion

Chief among the aims of this chapter is to provide a foundational framework for what moral judgment is and what it hangs upon for a dependable conclusion. For moral judgments are conclusions about whether a human act is right or wrong. If one believes there is no recipe for right and wrong determinations, then the activity of moral judgment is moot and even absurd. However, for most of recorded history, moral judgments have been made unreservedly and without equivocation. It is only in the modern and post-modern world that questions and critiques about moral judgment have arisen, from the mind of the business mentality of the libertarian, to the radical liberality of those who claim that moral consensus is a convenience to those in power or mere inventions to keep the population in control, to the push to abolish all morality and its determination because these practices are not effective nor respectful to those who disagree no matter how wrong they are. In light of this, the chapter compares those that propose and adhere to the wisdom of a world suspicious of moral relativity and, by contrast, those yearning for the objective truth posed by Jesus Christ.

Chapter 1 Endnotes

1   See: Timothy L. S. Sprigge, "Definition of a Moral Judgment," *Philosophy* 39, no. 150 (Oct. 1964): 301–322, https://doi.org/10.1017/S0031819100055777; Bertram F. Malle, "Moral Judgments," *Annual Review of Psychology* 72 (2021): 293–318, https://doi.org/10.1146/annurev-psych-072220-104358,https://www.cogsci.msu.edu/DSS/2021-2022/Malle/Malle%20(2021)%20Moral%20Judgments.pdf

2   Bernard Gert, "Moral Judgments," in *Morality: Its Nature and Justification* (Oxford University Press, 2005), https://doi.org/10.1093/0195176898.003.0012.

3   See: David G. Kirchhoffer, "Benedict XVI, Human Dignity, and Absolute Moral Norms," *New Blackfriars* 91, no. 1035 (2010): 586–608, http://www.jstor.org/stable/43251436.

4   James Q. Wilson, *Moral Judgment* (Basic Books, 1997); see also: Philip Selznick, review of "Moral Judgement: Does the Abuse Excuse Threaten our Legal System?" by James Q. Wilson, *The Wilson Quarterly*, http://archive.wilsonquarterly.com/book-reviews/moral-judgment-does-abuse-excuse-threaten-our-legal-system.

5   Mt 7:1 (NRSVCE).

6   Nathan Schleuter, "Libertarian Delusions: Exposing the Flaws in Libertarian Thinking," *First Things* (August/September 2014), https://www.firstthings.com/article/2014/08/libertarian-delusions.

7   Jason Brennan, "A Moral Pluralist Case for Libertarianism," Libertarianism.org, January 3, 2017, https://www.libertarianism.org/publications/essays/moral-pluralist-case-libertarianism.

8   John Paul II, *Veritatis Splendor*, August. 6, 1993, https://www.vatican.va/content/john-paul-ii/en/encyclicals/documents/hf_jp-ii_enc_06081993_veritatis-splendor.html.

9   *Veritatis*, ¶ 32.

10 See: Hanno Sauer, "Against Moral Judgment. The Empirical Case for Moral Abolitionism," *Philosophical Explorations* 24, no. 2 (2021): 137–54, https://doi:10.1080/13869795.2021.1908580.

11 See: R. Garner, "Morality: The Final Delusion?" *Philosophy Now* 82 (2011): 18–20.

12 See: Jennifer Cole Wright and Thomas Pölzler, "Should Morality Be Abolished? An Empirical Challenge to the Argument from Intolerance,"

Philosophical Psychology 35, no. 3 (2021): 350–385, https://doi.org/10.1080/09515089.2021.1983160.

13 See: Adam M. Mastroianna and Daniel T. Gilgert, "The Illusion of Moral Decline," *Nature* 618 (2023): 782–789, https://doi.org/10.1038/s41586-023-06137-x; Sauer, "Against Moral Judgment."

14 Joshua J. McElwee, "Francis Explains, 'Who Am I To Judge?'" National Catholic Reporter, January 10, 2016, https://www.ncronline.org/francis-explains-who-am-i-judge.

15 McElwee, "Francis Explains."

16 McElwee, "Francis Explains."

17 Cindy Wooden, "Doctrinal Dicastery Explains How, When Gay Couples Can Be Blessed," U.S. Conference of Catholic Bishops, December 18, 2023, https://www.usccb.org/news/2023/doctrinal-dicastery-explains-how-when-gay-couples-can-be-blessed.

18 See: Synodal Forum IV, presentation on "Life in succeeding relationships—Living love in sexuality and partnership" for the Second Reading at the Fifth Synodal Assembly (9–11 March 2023) for the implementation text "Blessing ceremonies for couples who love each other," https://www.synodalerweg.de/fileadmin/Synodalerweg/Dokumente_Reden_Beitraege/englisch-SV-V/ENG_SV-V-Synodalforum-IV Handlungstext.SegensfeiernFuerPaareDieSichLieben_Les2.pdf.

19 "Pope Francis' Letter Expressing Concern About German Synodal Way," National Catholic Register, November 10, 2023, https://www.ncregister.com/cna/full-text-pope-francis-letter-expressing-concern-about-german-synodal-way; see also: Jonathan Liedl, "Will the German Bishops Defy Pope Francis? All Eyes Are on Augsburg to Find Out," National Catholic Register, February 15, 2024, https://www.ncregister.com/news/will-the-german-bishops-defy-pope-francis-all-eyes-are-on-augsburg-to-find-out.

20 Mt 7:1 (DV).

21 Mt 7:2–5 (DV).

Chapter 2: Christ, Crime, and Moral Judgment

Introduction

While it is clear that contemporary perspectives are often confused, befuddled, and even wrong about the nature of moral judgment, it is important to reach some consensus on what moral judgment is. The possibilities of definition and evaluation are simply endless. Even so, a bit of consensus does emerge on what the act of moral judgment constitutes. Put simply, the act or process of moral judgment calls for an evaluation of human activity or a measure of its legitimacy and correctness. To morally evaluate assumes that a decision is reached concerning human action. Nothing here is very mystical, for the person who judges weighs two courses of action, at least roughly, and then picks or chooses the action consistent with our being and nature. Thus, the decision to kill another will be evaluated in light of particular criteria or variables, such as:

- Is the killing in time of war?
- Is the killing done in self-defense?
- Is the killing done under lawful authority?
- Are there alternatives to killing?
- What are the motivations for killing?

The list could be much longer, but, suffice it to say, the evaluation, assessment, and conclusions reached about why to kill edify the nature of moral judgment. And of course, the word "moral" causes consternation amongst those who tend to be amoral or the immoral or those that think that morality cannot be fixed in any context or that morals and morality are shaped by ruling classes, race theory, or economic status. In the twenty-first century, the term "moral" has become a mystery for many.[1]

Tied even more closely is how we judge—is it a rational exercise or a product of desire? Are judgments spurred on by passions, emotions, and personal preferences more than by rational deliberation?[2] That disagreement exists here is undeniable. However, most analysis of judgment tends to see reason and cognition as the chief tools for reaching conclusions about behavior. Even the psychological community, led by Lawrence Kohlberg and his followers, held that moral judgments are "primarily cognitive and a primary factor in the understanding of moral actions and emotions."[3]

Others have been pushing hard to explain moral judgment in largely biological terms by promoting the new "neuroscience" or moral judgment and decision making. Melanie Killen and Judith Smetana have made this a strong strand of their research, posing the following argument: *In an age of empiricism—these notions are quite attractive but whether sensibly part of the Christian view of moral judgment quite questionable.*[4] Still others conclude that moral judgments are merely reflections of the will and emotion alone, while others like Thomas Aquinas see moral reasoning and reasoning as largely the product of reason and rationality. It is reason that provides the knowledge of correct judgment; it is reason that lights the pathway to correct choices.

> Judgment is only possible by rational, intellectual creatures since it is the rational being who has ends and objects. These objects, these ends, from the finite to the infinite, so frequently referenced in St. Thomas' work, serve as the intellectual backdrop in human judgment. In the *Summa Contra Gentiles*, Thomas types each and every human activity "for the sake of some perfection."

The human agent intends to bring about perfection, but this is utterly unlikely if the skill at making sound judgments is absent. Judgment calls upon the human player to deliberate and decide, to counsel and select, to choose and discard any series of options. Judgment, in order to be correct, needs to conform to right reason and to its necessary, self-evident principles as its starting point.[5]

In this way, Thomas will lay out an objective, fixed reality of moral propositions grounded and rooted in reason—a part of the human purpose further aided and buttressed with the content of the natural law. This latter addition makes moral judgment dependable if we at least follow its instructions. Donald DeMarco, writing in the National Catholic Register, appreciates the correlation between natural law, its self-evident principles, and the Thomistic concept of judgment:

> The natural law offers us a reliable basis for making moral judgments. The ultimate purpose of education is to develop our inherent capacities to distinguish between truth and error. Being open-minded does not mean to remain open even when convincing evidence has been presented. The truly open-minded person remains open to the truth until he apprehends it.[6]

For Thomas, moral reasoning and the process of making moral judgments are intellectual exercises over all other parts of the human person. And in his schema of moral judgment, the step-by-step assessment depends primarily, though not exclusively, on the thinking, reasoning being. To reach a moral judgment on particular conduct, the player must:

- deliberate
- counsel and select
- choose or discard

Although intellect and reason identify the appropriate way of making moral judgments, free beings known as Homo sapiens can surely make the wrong decision and choose the errant option. Of course, this the power of will must be coupled with the knowledge of what to choose and what one chooses. Aquinas articulately poses the dilemma:

> For man can will and not will, act and not act; and again, he can will this or that, and do this or that. The reason for this is to be found in the very power of the reason. For the will can tend to whatever the reason can apprehend as good.[7]

As a result of this process, moral judgments require some significant deliberation, that is, thinking about options and alternatives.

> Now in things doubtful and uncertain, the reason does not pronounce judgment without previous inquiry. Therefore the reason must of necessity institute an inquiry before deciding on what is to be chosen; and this inquiry is called counsel.[8]

The Thomist perspective on moral judgment is a rich examination of human freedom, linking both reason and will with reason above all and, in the end, all of human choices.[9] In the final analysis, moral judgment will be dependable if and only when it is "intricately wed to reason and rationality."[10] The alternatives to reason are a bevy of relativistic and unpredictable variables that cannot generate a moral order. "Consciously or not, the human actor lives in a world of judgment. By nature, judgment is the undeniable by-product of reason discovering ends, deliberating and counseling internally over their content, and then willing the means, by consent, election, and application."[11] "Deliberation," Thomas declares, "can and should result in a chosen activity, a selected means to the ends, but said deliberation may or may not evolve into human activity. Indeed, St. Thomas signals that deliberation and counsel imply a resolution by their very nature, but implication is no guarantee. "Mindless, purposeless inquiry is contrary to the end of judgment since judgement is about resolution which leads to what must be done."[12]"[13]

Surely, when evaluating the Savior, Jesus Christ, the means and methods of moral scrutiny and judgment seem almost trivial. What is clear, however, is that Christ's judgments are not willy-nilly, arbitrary, or without fixture but rather something permanently true in all cases. The moral philosophy of Jesus Christ is not only dependable—it is perfect and unassailable. But this is not merely because of His Divinity but more so the result of His absolute perfection in all things. Even more compellingly, Jesus does not issue decrees or conclusions in a theological vacuum but is ready, willing, and forever able to apply moral truths to any particular situation. The Jesus who loves everyone and in every situation may be true in an ontological sense, though it is surely not the case in moral application. Jesus Christ loves all Creation yet is still capable of zeroing in on human activity that runs contrary to universal truth, the good, and the precepts of the natural law.

What follows are some general observations on why Jesus Christ, the Son of God, does not refrain from judgment but instead, confidently judges in a variety of settings. This side of Jesus, contrary to the happy-clappy, completely tolerant without a scintilla of judgment version, is the more accurate one.

Christ and the Proof of Moral Judgment

Even before his entry into the world, John the Baptist announced the coming of the Messiah. It was just not his coming that foretold his ultimate end and purpose. He was also a siren call to the culture, to humankind, to get straight with God and self-examine their shortcomings and failures. This is significant for two reasons:

First, if judgment were not at the centerpiece of Christ's coming, there really is no point in coming; and secondly, if John the Baptist were simply making announcements about the coming Son of God, he would have left it at that. Instead, John announces both the coming and the reason for it. John proclaimed: See Figure 2.

Caption: *The Baptism of Christ* by Nicolás Enríquez, 1773

> I baptize you with water for repentance, but he who is
> coming after me is mightier than I … His winnowing
> fork is in his hand, and he will clear his threshing floor
> and gather his wheat into the barn, but the chaff he
> will burn with unquenchable fire.[14]

The visual imagery is stark enough, and any allusions regarding a happy-go-lucky Jesus should be discarded. In this warning, John expressly calls for "repentance," and with repentance comes the assumption of wrong or error in the lives of Christians. Repentance imputes and expressly assumes that some behaviors are not to be tolerated and deserve condemnation. This is not the only warning of the Baptist; another is given when John proclaims:

> Even now the axe is laid to the root of the trees. Every
> tree therefore that does not bear good fruit is cut down
> and thrown into the fire.[15]

As in the other passage, such draconian language is not the stuff of endless tolerance and a willingness never to condemn or judge. Those who eschew the approach of the Baptist would prop up a Jesus with an overflowing cistern of tolerance. By tolerance we mean one can either avoid judgment or one can defer making a judgment. In Donald DiMarco's editorial, "Is Tolerance a Virtue?" he cuts to the essence of it:

> Tolerance lies sometimes between condemnation and
> approval. It operates within a spacious territory that
> ranges from tolerating another person's peculiar way of
> … to tolerating an injustice … But it becomes an issue
> when by it a person does nothing in the face of evil.[16]

In this landscape, neither the Baptist nor Jesus finds a home. To tolerate and exude tolerance, DiMarco aptly explains, "refrains from action … and backs away from acting."[17] Jesus never refrains from action and its evaluation.

In short, the overly tolerant lack both the intellect and will to make judgments and feel greater comfort in the avoidance of the dilemma. This framework is precisely why moral toleration turns into great injustice. The Holocaust mirrors the lack of moral judgment in a large swathe of one of the West's greatest cultures. The same could be said for the horrid legacy of *Roe v. Wade*[18] where innocents have perished in incalculable numbers. While most people are averse to abortion on the day of birth and delivery, something now demanded by the extreme abortion lobby, how can there be silence at this stage? How is extreme late term abortion distinguished from historical infanticide? Or what of the gender altering surgeries now taking place—or drag queen story hour for small children in today's libraries—how can these harmful activities be tolerated? It is the culture of toleration that not only assures that these perverse activities continue but guarantees many more in the near future.

Thankfully, the philosophy of Jesus Christ, while it can be and is forever forgiving, would not tolerate these actions. His entire purpose of entering into human form, His crucifixion and suffering, was not done in an environment of complete tolerance but the Father's recognition that His Son could be the Savior of the world. His very Incarnation was grounded, not in avoidance of sin and error, but the full embrace of Salvation History. In the Gospel of John, this purpose is clear enough:

> Indeed, God did not send the Son into the world to condemn the world, but in order that the world might be saved through him. Those who believe in him are not condemned; but those who do not believe are condemned already, because they have not believed in the name of the only Son of God. And this is the judgement,

that the light has come into the world, and people loved
darkness rather than light because their deeds were evil.
For all who do evil hate the light and do not come to
the light, so that their deeds may not be exposed.[19]

In another verse in the Gospel of John, Jesus proclaims the
reason He came into the world: "I have come as light into the
world, that whoever believes in me may not remain in darkness."[20]
"Jesus said to her, 'I am the resurrection and the life. Those who
believe in me, even though they die, will live, and everyone who
lives and believes in me will never die.'"[21]

Any reasoned examination of Christ recurringly comes back
to His role in our salvation. If all things were fine with the status
quo, with the rages of sin and error in human life, Salvation History would be an empty exercise. Because of this, we discover that
judgment provides a foundational rationalization for Christ's Incarnation.

A few other forms of proof confirm and corroborate the central role of moral judgment in Christian tradition, especially the
existence of Hell.

Hell and Its Centrality in Christ's Moral Judgment

A cursory reading of the New Testament makes evident that Hell is
not a rumor nor a creative invention, but a very real locus reserved
for those who neither accept Christ nor keep His teachings close or
fail to be obedient to His commandments. There are literally hun-
dreds of references to this anguished place in the afterlife—many of
which are directly referenced by Jesus Himself. On its face, Hell is
the direct result of moral judgment; for to go there, or in the opposite direction, towards Heaven, requires a moral judgment—a conclusion that a person deserves one place or the other. Without the
continuum of good human acts from bad or malicious human

activity, it becomes impossible for one to distinguish good from evil. Without this distinction, moral reasoning and moral judgment become futile exercises. Without Hell or Heaven, why measure differences in human behavior? Jesus warns the world to see what is coming around the bend for those who live in sin and error when He says, "Repent, for the kingdom of heaven is at hand."[22]

At the same time, Jesus makes plain that judgment inevitably resides in His Father, who shall call each human being to account and evaluate the quality or lack thereof in his or her human existence. However, as human agents, it is essential that we prepare for the eventuality of Heaven and Hell—that we live our lives dutifully and virtuously, in accordance with the tenets of the natural law and spiritual law of God. We are more than floating flotsam awaiting divine judgment. Accordingly, human conduct and corresponding choices of human action must be evaluated day to day. In Matthew's Gospel, Jesus unequivocally makes clear that "the Son of Man will send his angels, and they will gather out of his kingdom all causes of sin and all evildoers."[23] In addition to being gathered, these same evildoers shall be thrown in "the furnace of fire, where there will be weeping and gnashing of teeth."[24]

Jesus can be stunningly direct on this topic, and He has no reservations in confirming that there will be a place of fire and anguish reserved for those who do not heed His teachings. One of the more compelling affirmations of Hell can be found in Matthew's Gospel:

> Then he will say to those on his left, "Depart from me, you accursed, into the eternal fire prepared for the devil and his angels. For I was hungry, and you did not give me anything to eat; I was thirsty, and you did not give me anything to drink; I was a stranger, and you did not welcome me; I was naked, and you did not give me any clothing; I was ill and in prison and you did not visit

me." Then they will ask him, "Lord, when did we see you hungry or thirsty or a stranger or naked or ill or in prison and not minister to you?" He will answer them, "Amen, I say to you, whatever you failed to do for one of the least of these brethren of mine, you failed to do for me." And they will go away to eternal punishment, but the righteous will enter eternal life.[25]

Equivocation does not occur to Jesus when speaking of Hell, for He is so convinced of its existence that He tells His followers it is better to lose an organ of the body, like an arm, an eye, or ear, than allow temptation to corrupt one's soul. Jesus states:

> If your right eye causes you to sin, pluck it out and throw it away; it is better that you lose one of your members than that your whole body be thrown into hell. And if your right hand causes you to sin, cut it off and throw it away; it is better that you lose one of your members than that your whole body go into hell.[26]

In the Gospel of Mark, Jesus refers to the "unquenchable fire" as a place for those who fail to keep the teachings of the Father.

> And if your hand causes you to sin, cut it off; it is better for you to enter life maimed than with two hands to go to hell, to the unquenchable fire. And if your foot causes you to sin, cut it off; it is better for you to enter life lame than with two feet to be thrown into hell. And if your eye causes you to sin, pluck it out; it is better for you to enter the kingdom of God with one eye than with two eyes to be thrown into hell, where their worm does not die, and the fire is not quenched.[27]

Christ's instructions are emphatically clear: obey or suffer the consequences; and, in this sense, the ebb and flow of moral judgment is unimpeded. Throughout the Gospels, Christ references a place of punishment and the extremely negative consequence of sin rather than some tolerant and boundlessly merciful setting that many in the mainstream Churches promote. Even Pope Francis was caught being ambiguous about Hell—although subsequent denials from the Vatican immediately followed. In a 2024 interview, he remarked on whether God forgives everyone:

> It's difficult to imagine it. What I would say is not a dogma of faith, but my personal thought: I like to think hell is empty; I hope it is.[28]

Is it any wonder the Pope's statement caused such an uproar? For Jesus, there is no such ambiguity, but repeated affirmations of a place called Hell. In the Gospel of Luke, Jesus declares:

> And some one said to him, "Lord, will those who are saved be few?" And he said to them, "Strive to enter by the narrow door; for many, I tell you, will seek to enter and will not be able."[29]

The contrast between the Papal observation and Christ's description of the challenge of eternal life and the existence of a Hell could not be more vivid. In well-meaning people, there is this undeniable attraction to mercy without limits—that God will be perpetually forgiving and gracious enough to allow sin and failure to dissipate without consequence. This approach is surely not that of Jesus Christ. Jesus is much more realistic about human behavior that goes unchecked and lacks consequences. In Matthew He comments:

A sound tree cannot bear evil fruit, nor can a bad tree bear good fruit. Every tree that does not bear good fruit is cut down and thrown into the fire.[30]

Jesus further comments that the path to destruction is more readily achieved than the "hard" path to life espoused by His followers. He notes:

Enter by the narrow gate; for the gate is wide and the way is easy, that leads to destruction, and those who enter by it are many. For the gate is narrow and the way is hard, that leads to life, and those who find it are few.[31]

If everything were so readily achievable by all and in all circumstances, without condemnation of any sort, then moral judgment would lack all meaning. In its place, Jesus sets up a system of making moral judgments that are adjudged by the will and desire of the Father and for those who maintain and uphold tradition. For Christ, the matter of moral judgement is inexorably tied to human action and human conduct which is compatible with the law of the Father, the virtues, and truth. Not everything the human agent undertakes goes toward this realm. Some conduct reaps reward, and other conduct reaps negative punishment. Jesus is not hesitant to cast out those who fail to adhere to His principles and those of His Father. In the Gospel of Matthew, He shows a complete and unbridled willingness to reserve Heaven to those who deserve it and equally willing to assign placement in Hell to those who have earned it by their deeds.

Be on guard against false prophets who come to you disguised in sheep's clothing, but who inwardly are ravenous wolves. By their fruits you will know them. Does one pick grapes from thornbushes or figs from thistles? In the same way, every good tree bears good fruit, but a rotten tree produces bad fruit. A good tree cannot bear bad fruit, nor can a bad tree bear good fruit. Every tree that does not bear good fruit is cut down and thrown into the fire. Thus, by their fruits you will know them.

Not everyone who says to me, "Lord, Lord," will enter the kingdom of heaven, but only the one who does the will of my heavenly Father. Many will say to me on that day, "Lord, Lord, did we not prophesy in your name? Did we not drive out demons in your name? Did we not perform many miracles in your name?" Then I will tell them plainly, "I never knew you. Depart from me, you evildoers!"[32]

See Figure 3.

Throughout His many parables and discourses, Jesus reiterates these same themes—that the world must reward the good and punish the evildoers. At no place is this more determined than His judgment of those who would harm children. In this realm, the protection and care of children, Jesus manifests His special love for the little ones amongst us. One should visit and revisit these words when considering how poorly the Church has done in the matter of child sexual abuse cases. Christ displays no hesitation, for He makes His judgment and makes it without excuse, mitigation, or defense when it comes to the protection of children. Anyone who doubts the capacity and power of Christ to make moral judgments must visit and revisit these words:

> Whoever causes one of these little ones who believe in me to sin, it would be better for him if a great millstone were hung round his neck, and he were thrown into the sea.[33]

Conclusion

Those who doubt Christ's capacity to morally judge human action, and at the same time to dole out consequences for those actions, either has yet to read His words or chosen to selectively disregard them. In Christ's very Incarnation, the essence of judgment is fully encapsulated, for Salvation History is not an empty promise nor some informal messaging, but a plan of salvation shaped and crafted by the Heavenly Father to redeem a very corrupt and errant world. In short, salvation and moral judgment go hand in hand in their aim and purpose, for without judgment the measure for worthiness or not simply does not exist.

Just as critically, Christ's measure of moral judgment depends upon some self-evident principles rooted in natural law thinking and encompasses the Law of the Prophets, the Ten Commandments, and the laws that provide for collective tranquility and individual flourishing. There are no signs of moral relativity in the philosophy of Jesus Christ.

As a result of this, His judgments have consequences—the most primordial consequence being where one ends up in the afterlife—in either Heaven or Hell. The contemporary caricature of Jesus is as an endless font of an unbridled mercy without ends or limits. If this is the case, His discourses on Hell would lack all sensibility when the very opposite is true; for Christ keenly, articulately, and precisely describes Hell as reserved for those who do not adhere to His teachings or those of His Father.

Finally, the chapter affirms how personal culpability and responsibility are not matters of deterministic whims and societal pressures, but a matter of choice and free will. Christ adheres to a view of a human person, fully enunciated by Aquinas and others, who is free, can discern right from wrong, and has an intellect and reason to discover what is true and right.

Chapter 2 Endnotes

1   David Sackris and Rasmus Rosenberg Larsen, "Are There Moral Judgments?" *European Journal of Analytic Philosophy* 19, no. 1 (2023): 1–23; see also: Wilson, *Moral Judgment*.

2   *Catechism of the Catholic Church*, 2nd ed. (United States Catholic Conference, 2000), § 1767, https://www.vatican.va/content/catechism/en/part_three/section_one/chapter_one/article_5/ii_passions_and_moral_life.html.

3   Stephen J. Thomas and Yangxue Dong, "The Defining Issues Test of Moral Judgment Development," *Behavioral Development Bulletin* 19, no. 3 (2014): 56, https://doi.org/10.1037/h0100590.

4   See: Joshua May, Clifford I. Workman, Julia Haas, and Hyemin Han, "The Neuroscience of Moral Judgment: Empirical and Philosophical Developments," in *Neuroscience and Philosophy*, ed. Felipe De Brigard and Walter Sinnott-Armstrong (MIT Press, 2022); see also: Keith Humphreys, "Of Moral Judgments and Sexual Addiction," *Addiction* 113, no. 3 (March 2018): 387–388.

5   Charles P. Nemeth, *Aquinas in the Courtroom: Lawyers, Judges, and Judicial Conduct* (Praeger Press, 2001), 115–116.

6   Donald DeMarco, "To Judge or Not to Judge?" National Catholic Register, June 17, 2024, https://www.ncregister.com/commentaries/judge-or-not-to-judge-demarco.

7   Thomas Aquinas, "Summa Theologica," in *Basic Writings of Saint Thomas Aquinas*, ed. Anton C. Pegis, vol. 2 (Random House, 1945), I-II, Q. 13, a. 6, c.

8   Aquinas, "Summa Theologica," I-II, Q. 14, a. 1, c.

9   See: Judith A. Barad, "Aquinas on the Role of Emotion in Moral Judgment and Activity," *The Thomist* 55, no. 3 (July 1991): 397–413, https://doi.org/ 10.1353/tho.1991.0007; David T. Echelbarger, "Aquinas on the Passions: Contribution to Moral Reasoning," Proceedings of the American Catholic Philosophical Association 86 (2012): 281–293, https://doi.org/10.5840/acpaproc20128622.

10   Nemeth, *Aquinas in the Courtroom*, 123.

11   Nemeth, *Aquinas in the Courtroom*, 122

12   Aquinas, "Summa Theologica," I-II, Q. 14, a. 5, c.

13   Nemeth, Aquinas in the Courtroom, 118.

14   Mt 3:11–12 (ESV).

15   Mt 3:10 (ESV).

16   Donald DiMarco, "Is Tolerance a Virtue?" *The Wanderer* 157, no. 27, (July 4, 2024): 4A.

17   DiMarco, "Is Tolerance a Virtue?" 4A.

18   410 U.S. 113 (1973).

19   Jn 3:17–20 (NRSVACE).

20   Jn 12:46 (NHEB).

21   Jn 11:25–26 (NRSVACE).

22   Mt 4:17 (NKJV).

23   Mt 13:41 (RSV).

24   Mt 13:42 (RSV).

25   Mt 25:41–46 (NCB).

26   Mt 5:29–30 (RSVCE).

27   Mk 9:43–48 (RSVCE).

28   See Cindy Wooden, "Pope Francis Says He Hopes Hell Is 'Empty,'" *America Magazine*, January 15, 2024, https://www.americamagazine.org/faith/2024/01/15/pope-francis-resign-interview-246936.

29 Lk 13:23–24 (RSVCE).
30 Mt 7:18–19 (RSVCE).
31 Mt 7:13–14 (RSVCE).
32 Mt 7:15–23 (NCB).
33 Mk 9:42 (RSVCE).

Chapter 3: Christ, the Decalogue, and a Crimes Code

Introduction

Part of the rationale for this work is rooted in the question of Christ's practice and perfection of moral judgment. Too often Jesus has been typecast or caricatured as a sort of "Purple Barney" figure with the ditty, "I love you—you love me, and we are a happy family." By no means do I wish to critique the importance or goodness of the figure children so commonly encounter; on the other hand, it seems almost a falsehood to reduce Jesus Christ to being nothing more than an endless fountain of forgiveness. In any honest reading of the New Testament—and in the words of Jesus Himself—we do find perfect love and care for all His creation, and while these attributes are to be emulated, in both word and action, we often encounter a Jesus willing to call out things not right. The closer and more intimately we read the language of the Savior, something else emerges—a sort of criminal code that is both derived from the Jewish faith but, at the same time, imbued with some of the more brilliant aspects of Roman law.

Throughout all four Gospels, the reader encounters legal principles and maxims, definitions on common legal dilemmas, like usury or debt, taxes and the consequence of evasion, and the distinction between public and private authority in the matter of law and punishment to name a few. The biggest surprise, however, is that Christ promulgates a crimes code—a code that includes many traditional offenses we commonly encounter in contemporary settings. By no measure is it a fully complete codification, like a state criminal code or the Model Penal Code, yet its breadth and depth is quite revealing. From murder to assault, adultery to fornication, theft and fraud, as illustrations, the New Testament's content, and the express language of Jesus Himself, develops an identifiable criminal jurisprudence.

Christ, Crime, and the Decalogue

At the foundation of this inquiry rests Christ's affirmation of His fulfillment of the Old Testament and those who foretold His coming. Throughout the Old Testament, there are references to the coming Messiah. In the Book of Isaiah, His coming is grippingly foretold:

> For to us a child is born, to us a son is given, and the government will be on his shoulders.
> And he will be called Wonderful Counselor, Mighty God, Everlasting Father, Prince of Peace.
> Of the increase of his government and peace there will be no end.
> He will reign on David's throne and over his kingdom, establishing and upholding it with justice and righteousness from that time on and forever.
> The zeal of the Lord Almighty will accomplish this.[1]

Just as compelling, in the Book of Psalms, the reference to Jesus coming to be amongst us is clear enough:

> I will proclaim the decree of the LORD:
> He said to me, "You are my Son;
> today I have become your Father."[2]

These passages simply corroborate a prophetic story about Jesus and why the Father sent His Son: to deliver us from evil and

sin, to be a propitiation for our fallen state, and to open the doors
to the Kingdom of Heaven. Interestingly, Jesus often tells His disciples and those who listen that His mission and aim is neither an
optional nor discretionary pick, but instead a formal appointment
by His Father to oversee both Heaven and earth. In Matthew's
Gospel, Jesus claims His status as one in "authority":

> Then Jesus came to them and said, "All authority in heaven
> and on earth has been given to me. Therefore, go and make
> disciples of all nations, baptizing them in the name of the
> Father and of the Son and of the Holy Spirit, and teaching
> them to obey everything I have commanded you. And
> surely, I am with you always, to the very end of the age."[3]

The importance of the continuity between prophecy, the
salvific history attributed to the Son of God, and how inexorably
bound Jesus is to the faith of His forefathers cannot be over-em-
phasized. Nowhere do we encounter a Jesus who wishes to lay
waste to what preceded Him. In fact, we continuously find Jesus
telling His followers to discern and discover the seamless continuity
between Him and those who foretold His Coming. Jesus does not
vanquish His Jewish traditions and roots, but rather fully integrates
their teaching into a philosophy of life and truth. Jesus is the fulfillment of the Law not its abolisher.

> Do not think that I have come to abolish the Law or
> the Prophets; I have not come to abolish them but to
> fulfill them. For I tell you the truth, until heaven and
> earth disappear, not the smallest letter, not the least
> stroke of a pen, will by any means disappear from the
> Law until everything is accomplished. Anyone who
> breaks one of the least of these commandments and
> teaches others to do the same will be called least in the

kingdom of heaven, but whoever practices and teaches these commands will be called great in the kingdom of heaven. For I tell you that unless your righteousness surpasses that of the Pharisees and the teachers of the law, you will certainly not enter the kingdom of heaven.[4]

In this passage, Jesus affirms the integrity and the continuity of the Law of the Prophets and urges His followers to stay true to the Law espoused in this form and His new emphasis on love and charity. Add to this, His reference again to the consequences of not following the Law or following it for all the wrong reasons, such as His critique of the Pharisees. As in so many other contexts, the doorway, the pathway, the reception to those who fail to follow the Law will remain narrow and even closed.

For truly, I say to you, till heaven and earth pass away, not an iota, not a dot, will pass from the law until all is accomplished.[5]

At no place will the emphasis on continuity be stronger than in His affirmation of the Decalogue—the Ten Commandments. Even in the American experience, many foundational interpreters of the documents that launched this nation have indicated that these same Ten Commandments are a building block for a civilized nation-state and a formula and recipe for a healthy citizenry.[6]

These same Ten Commandments used to be emblazoned on courthouses, schoolhouses, government installations, and a host of other settings.[7] The Ten Commandments served as a minimalist yet extremely powerful list of do's and don'ts for the American democratic and republican form.[8]

The Louisiana legislation to reinstall the Ten Commandment in all schools has caused hyperventilation and angst in abolishers of these once well-entrenched commands in Western culture. The law reads in part:

§1283. Context of public display

Public displays set forth in R.S. 25:1282(B), (C), (D), and (E) shall be accompanied by a document entitled "Context for Acknowledging America's Religious History" which shall read as follows:

(1) Some documents stand out as pivotal in the religious history of America and Louisiana's legal system, among which are the Mayflower Compact, the Declaration of Independence as a legal foundation for the United States Constitution, the Ten Commandments as one of the foundations of our legal system, and the Northwest Ordinance, which was a primary document affirming faith and the first congressional act legally prohibiting slavery. It is hoped that their study and relation to each other and the history of our state and nation will foster an appreciation for the role that religion has played in the legal history of America and the state of Louisiana and prompt further public study.

(2) American law, constitutionalism, and political theory have deep roots in religion. American ideals about liberty, freedom, equality, legal responsibility, and codes of law, to mention a few, have roots and underpinnings in religion and biblical literacy. The Ten Commandments, which are found in the Book of Exodus in the Old Testament of the Bible, was one of the earliest written expressions of law to be incorporated in American legal systems. The Ten Commandments, or the law of nature, also impacted the Declaration of Independence which refers to the "laws of nature and of Nature's God."[9]

As in Louisiana, during Christ's tenure on this earth, the Ten Commandments were referenced and cited with regularity and confidence. Jesus never veers far from the Ten Commandments. Why would He or should He? Nothing in the commands is anything but beneficial to individuals and the common good. Nothing in the prescribed rules and demands could undermine a civilization or destroy its citizenry.[10]

Indeed, it can readily be argued that the faster our abandonment of them, the faster our decline. Since the purge of the Ten Commandments commenced in the 1960's, our culture has coarsened, our crime rates have skyrocketed, our families disintegrated, and our substance abuse and mental health data has pushed to incalculable levels.

Why such vociferous objections when Christ Himself held firm to its content? Weigh and evaluate the contents of the Commandments—where does it lead us astray? See Figure 4.[11]

The Ten Commandments

1. You shall have no other gods before me.

2. You shall not make for yourself an image in the form of anything in heaven above or on the earth beneath or in the waters below. You shall not bow down to them or worship them; for I, the LORD your God, am a jealous God, punishing the children for the sin of the parents to the third and fourth generation of those who hate me, but showing love to a thousand generations of those who love me and keep my commandments.

3. You shall not misuse the name of the LORD your God, for the LORD will not hold anyone guiltless who misuses his name.

4. Remember the Sabbath day by keeping it holy. Six days you shall labor and do all your work, but the seventh day is a sabbath to the LORD your God. On it you shall not do any work, neither you, nor your son or daughter, nor your male or female servant, nor your animals, nor any foreigner residing in your towns. For in six days the LORD made the heavens and the earth, the sea, and all that is in them, but he rested on the seventh day. Therefore, the LORD blessed the Sabbath day and made it holy.

5. Honor your father and your mother, so that you may live long in the land the LORD your God is giving you.

6. You shall not murder.

7. You shall not commit adultery.

8. You shall not steal.

9. You shall not give false testimony against your neighbor.

10. You shall not covet your neighbor's house. You shall not covet your neighbor's wife, or his male or female servant, his ox or donkey, or anything that belongs to your neighbor.

In terms of crime and criminality, the Decalogue richly defines and delineates proscribed behavior. Though the earlier three Commandments relative to the worshiping of the one true God, the avoidance of idols, idolatrous images, and false gods, as well as profanity in the use of God's name, would seem to the contemporary citizen irrelevant and unrelated to criminal codifications, this has not always been the case. During the magnificent empires of Rome and Greece, spiritual life and religious expression were central to governance. Even though pagan by design, the role of religion was tightly bound to the success of these empires.[12] And during the time of Jesus, the Jewish structure of life and politics, governance and discipline were passionately tied to faith and Talmudic doctrine. In Jewish culture, the Ten Commandments were a treasured and revered document. Hence, punishing violations and affronts to God, both as to His Being and in the method and manner of worship, or failing to adhere to regulations and guidelines, was utterly normative. Breaking those rules could result in serious punishments. Jesus Himself was wrongfully accused of blasphemy—a death penalty offense during His time. In the Gospel of Mark, Jesus's claim that He was the Son of God was met with the threat of death.

> "You have heard the blasphemy. What do you think?"
> They all condemned him as worthy of death.[13]

In Matthew, the dramatic action of the High Priest tearing his shirt underscores the seriousness of the charge.

> Then the high priest tore his clothes and said, "He has spoken blasphemy! Why do we need any more witnesses? Look, now you have heard blasphemy."[14]

See Figure 5 on the following page.

Until the late nineteenth century, even into parts of the twentieth, in the American experience, blasphemy could be discovered in criminal codes as could failing to keep a day of rest on the Sabbath. Profanity was also criminalized, as were a host of other offenses involving religious practice and the spiritual life. A clear example of this were state "Blue Laws," where liquor could not be sold on Sundays and stores were not permitted to operate on Sunday.[15]

And do not assume that all of these once very entrenched laws are no longer part of the legal landscape. An illustration of the laws that harken back to another time would be the current Mississippi law on cursing:

Current as of January 01, 2023
If any person shall profanely swear or curse, or use vulgar and indecent language, or be drunk in any public

place, in the presence of two (2) or more persons, he shall, on conviction thereof, be fined not more than one hundred dollars ($100.00) or be imprisoned in the county jail not more than thirty (30) days or both.[16]

Outside of the Decalogue's religious dimension resides a series of traditional felonies and misdemeanors that modern culture has become accustomed to. Christ was equally familiar with this content and never hesitates to cite the ad seriatim listing of the Ten Commandments.

> It is what comes out of a person that defiles. For it is from within, from the human heart, that evil intentions come: fornication, theft, murder, adultery, avarice, wickedness, deceit, licentiousness, envy, slander, pride, folly. All these evil things come from within, and they defile a person.[17]

Even more precisely, Jesus responds to His questioners with frequent references to the Commandments and how keeping them assures eternal life. In response to a follower wishing to know how to attain eternal life, Jesus says:

> "Why do you ask me about what is good? There is only one who is good. If you wish to enter into life, keep the commandments." He said to him, "Which ones?" And Jesus said, "You shall not murder; You shall not commit adultery; You shall not steal; You shall not bear false witness; Honor your father and mother; also, You shall love your neighbor as yourself."[18]

Jesus never displays any resistance or hesitation in upholding the tenets and precepts of the Decalogue. Its content constitutes the moral foundation for His teachings and overall philosophy and, just as keenly, manifests His deep and abiding affection for this sort of moral continuity, for the Commandments are a series of moral judgments. Each commandment issues a decision about human action, and each produces a singular answer. The Commandments are neither optional dicta nor relativistic principles that depend on culture, country, or individual inclinations. Similar to natural law reasoning and precepts, these instructions are to be universally applied in the same way one hopes a criminal codification would be.

A summary review of the type of crimes and infractions evident in the Commandments will prepare the reader for a closer look in subsequent chapters.

Fourth Commandment on the Sabbath: Blue Law Violations, Intoxication Restrictions and Disorderly Conduct

Fifth Commandment on Giving Honor to Parents: Incorrigible Behavior and Delinquency, Elder Abuse, Neglect, Fraud in Benefits for the Elderly, Misappropriation, Violations of Fiduciary Duty

Sixth Commandment on Killing: Murder, Manslaughter, Negligent Homicide, Infanticide, Suicide, Euthanasia, Sale of Controlled Substances Resulting in Death, Assault

Seventh Commandment on Adultery: Adultery, Fornication, Bigamy, Polygamy, Abuse of Spouse, Lewd and Lascivious Behavior, Licentiousness, Statutory Rape and Sodomy

Eight Commandment on Stealing: Theft and Larceny, Robbery, Pickpocketing, Fraud and Financial Crimes, Embezzlement and Extortion

Ninth Commandment on False Witness: Perjury, False Statements and Falsification, Misrepresentations, Libel, Slander and Defamation

Tenth Commandment on Covetousness: Theft and Misappropriation, Embezzlement, Fraud, Tax Evasion, Trespass and Malicious Destruction of Another's Property, Inordinate Compensatory Schemes when Compared to Business Financial Health, Breach of Fiduciary Duties

Over the next three chapters we shall delve into the particular criminal offenses, derived from the Decalogue, that were examined by Jesus. Accepting that the codification may not be as comprehensive as contemporary codes, the review will lay out and evaluate the crimes code of Jesus Christ—a place that provides a bedrock for future common law principles and modern-day legislation relating to the law of crimes.

Conclusion

This chapter stresses the integral role of the Ten Commandments, the Decalogue, as a foundational building block for definitions of crime. That the Decalogue is really a criminal codification is not puzzling for those who work in the law of crimes and are familiar with its content. The Decalogue essentially catalogs many of the major felonies and constitutes a central piece of the Old Law that Jesus comes not to abolish but to fulfill.

At another level, the chapter looks closely at how the law of crimes manifests itself in both the history and legacy of Jesus's times and religious influences. He supplements these long-held notions with His philosophy that both acknowledges the Old Law and combines it with the New Testament, an approach that was so ably communicated by Jesus to His followers. Aside from the Decalogue, Jesus makes plain that He does not come into the world to repeal the Old Law but to revitalize it and drive it towards its ultimate purpose.

Chapter 3 Endnotes

1   Is 9:6-7 (NIV).
2   Ps 2:7 (NIV).
3   Mt 28:18–20 (NIV).
4   Mt 5:17–20 (NIV).
5   Mt 5:18 (RSVCE).

6   See Steven K. Green, "The Fount of Everything Just and Right? The Ten Commandments as a Source of American Law," *Journal of Law and Religion* 14, no. 2 (1999–2000): 525–558, https://doi.org/ 10.2307/3556579.

7   Many have called for the end of these being displayed on any public building. See: Herbert Rothschild, "Relocation: Decline and Fall of the Ten Commandments," *Ashland News*, June 21, 2024, https://ashland.news/relocations-decline-and-fall-and-the-ten-commandments.

8   Kenyn Cureton, *Ten Commandments: Foundation of American Society* (Family Research Council, 2024), https://downloads.frc.org /EF/EF10I86.pdf.

9   La. Rev. Stat. § 25:1283 (2023).

10 Michael Youssef, "Faith & Liberty: What Our Founding Fathers Advocated for," *Leading the Way*, June 29, 2023, https://www.ltw.org/ read/articles/2023/07/faith-liberty-what-our-founding-fathers-advocated-for.

11 Image: Freepik.com. This image has been designed using assets from Freepik.com. Exodus 20 (NIV).

12 See: Cicero's *De Legibus* and Aristotle's *Nicomachean Ethics*.

13 Mk 14:64 (NIV).

14 Mt 26:65 (NIV).

15 For an interesting survey of presently existing Blue Laws, see: "Blue Laws by State: What are Sunday Blue Laws?" *TiPS*, January 26, 2023, https://www.gettips.com/blog/sunday-blue-laws.

16 Miss. Code § 97-29-47 (2024).

17 Mk 7:20–23 (NRSVCE).

18 Mt 19:17–19 (NRSVCE).

Chapter 4: Christ, Crime, and Moral Judgment: Murder and Other Bodily Offenses

Introduction

Thus far, we have examined the broader concepts of moral judgment gleaned from the words of Jesus Christ; and, by most measures, the idea of judgment and corresponding consequences comfortably resides in His philosophy on human action. At this juncture, our attention will turn to particular acts or offenses that even modern life defines and delineates as a "crime" and conduct which undermines the common good and the integrity of individuals. Although Jesus does not cover every criminal code provision modern society encounters, there is a good bit to digest in terms of criminal jurisprudence.

Side by side with this crime analysis and delineation will be the redemptive qualities of the Savior, Jesus Christ. Even in the darkest human behavior, Jesus leaves the door open to redemption and change, not only because of His profound and almost immeasurable mercy but also in our capacity to seek forgiveness and foster internal change. Even in the darkest of places—the prison, the jail, or the correctional facility—the troubled criminal inhabitants can find peace in the message of Jesus Christ. A highly successful program that deals with the prison criminal population, the Prison Fellowship Program, articulates its mission by declaring that Christ Himself was a prisoner in the Roman justice system.

Jesus personally understands prisoners. They are one of the least-reached groups in the world—cut off from society and left alone to cope with their feelings of anger, hopelessness, and despair. Jesus invites prisoners to join Him on a journey of hope, mercy, and forgiveness that will transform their hearts and minds from the inside out.

It can be easy to dismiss the idea of caring for prisoners and leave solutions to the government. But crime touches all of our communities, and prisoners are our neighbors. Jesus tells us it is imperative to our personal wholeness and the health of our communities to love our neighbors like we love ourselves.[1]

While the comparison of the Son of God, a completely innocent victim of the secular and civil justice system, is distinctly and radically different than the situation of most in the prison population, the message of Jesus Christ illuminates a very dark and troubled setting. In Christ, despite the level of criminality, there is enduring hope. As each criminal offense unfolds in the pages ahead, remember that Christ is the Way, the Truth, and the Life.

Christ on Murder

That Christ condemns the act of murder without justification or right is no surprise. One frequently encounters Jesus relying upon the express terms of the Decalogue and reiterating the Commandment, "Thou shall not kill." With extraordinary regularity, Jesus refers to the fundamental tenets of the Ten Commandments in responses to questions He receives. In the Gospel of Mark, Jesus responds as the Good Teacher:

As he was setting out on a journey, a man ran up and knelt before him, and asked him, "Good Teacher, what must I do to inherit eternal life?" Jesus said to him, "Why do you call me good? No one is good but God alone. You know the commandments: 'You shall not murder; You shall not commit adultery; You shall not steal; You shall not bear false witness; You shall not defraud; Honor your father and mother.'"[2]

Similarly in Luke, Jesus responds to the same question:

A certain ruler asked him, "Good Teacher, what must I do to inherit eternal life?" Jesus said to him, "Why do you call me good? No one is good but God alone. You know the commandments: 'You shall not commit adultery; You shall not murder; You shall not steal; You shall not bear false witness; Honor your father and mother.'"[3]

In Matthew, the admonition from Jesus is "You shall not kill."[4]

Aside from this express reliance on the Decalogue, Jesus paints a picture of murder that wraps and weaves its way throughout Salvation History. Manifesting His perfect knowledge, Jesus tells His followers that our understanding of murder, or of any other crime for that matter, has a long legal lineage. In Matthew, Jesus tells His follower that "You have heard that it was said to those of ancient times, 'You shall not murder;' and 'whoever murders shall be liable to judgment.'"[5]

See Figure 6 on the following page.

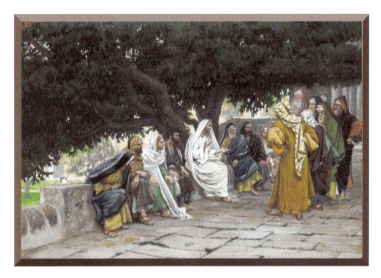

The Pharisees and Sadducees Come to Tempt Jesus by James Tissot, 1886

Yet despite these long-standing prohibitions of murder, Jesus scathingly attacks religious figures who have murdered while advocating their own holiness and religiosity. It is difficult to find more intense passages in the New Testament after reading Jesus's piercing condemnation of the Scribes and Pharisees, whom He directly indicts in matters of murder:

> Woe to you, scribes and Pharisees, hypocrites! For you build the tombs of the prophets and decorate the graves of the righteous, and you say, "If we had lived in the days of our ancestors, we would not have taken part with them in shedding the blood of the prophets." Thus, you testify against yourselves that you are descendants of those who murdered the prophets. Fill up, then, the measure of your ancestors. You snakes, you

brood of vipers! How can you escape being sentenced to hell? Therefore, I send you prophets, sages, and scribes, some of whom you will kill and crucify, and some you will flog in your synagogues and pursue from town to town.[6]

Interpretations vary as to the overall application of this condemnation, though no one who reads the words of Jesus can avoid noticing His fiery language and even His ultimate penalty being "Hell." By both implication and express language, Jesus displays a healthy anger towards those using a religious position of authority to carry out nefarious acts including murder. In this setting, Jesus is likely referring to the execution of John the Baptist, who prophesied the coming of Jesus Christ, and even more chillingly the words foretell His own execution in the days to come. By their participation, by their silence and lack of objection, a complicit picture of murder emerges. Indeed, these parties are aiders, abettors, and even accessories to murder.

For Jesus, those entrusted with spiritual salvation have a higher calling than the masses, and any descent into the malevolent world of murder cannot be brooked or tolerated. For this reason alone, Jesus confronts their hypocrisy with power, force, and justice.

Finally, Jesus correctly anticipates the contemporary definition of the crime of murder, namely that one must commit an act, that being murder or unlawful killing, which has been labeled the "Actus Reus." While the act is required, it is only the first part of two elements. Act must be coupled with intention or purpose. As we shall soon see, Christ insists upon proof of what comes from within.

Murder as an Intentional Act: From within the Person

Another extraordinary insight in the criminal jurisprudence of Jesus Christ encompasses what modern thinkers label "mens rea" or the mental component of the criminal act. To be guilty of a criminal charge, the burden of proof demands aligned confirmation of the actor's mental state. An act alone will not suffice.[7] For acts may be accidental or negligent, or an act can also be justifiable, such as in time of war and when done in self-defense. Proof of the act is the first step in the process. More complicated will be providing the proof of intentionality or, in some cases, an explanation as to motive or other thinking behind the killing. In short, what was the mind thinking and choosing at the time of the act? To kill in rage or commit premeditated murder or act with malicious forethought? For Jesus, the act has to be coupled with the mind. One can derive that conclusion from many parts of the New Testament. In the Gospel of Mark, His characterization of inner motivation as the defiling aspect could not be more probative.

> And he said, "It is what comes out of a person that defiles. For it is from within, from the human heart, that evil intentions come, fornication, theft, murder, adultery, avarice, wickedness, deceit, licentiousness, envy, slander, pride, folly. All these evil things come from within, and they defile a person."[8]

In Matthew, the same sentiment appears without waiver:

> For out of the heart come evil intentions, murder, adultery, fornication, theft, false witness, slander. These are what defile a person, but to eat with unwashed hands does not defile.[9]

Within this passage, Jesus prioritizes human actions that defile the person—not dietary violations. This constitutes a critique against overzealous leaders of the faith for their obsessive scrutiny of incidental legal matters. On the other hand, evil intentionality to kill another that comes from within clearly qualifies.

What a criminal actor intends or thinks can be broad in scope, and a picture of evil intent that rationalizes the sense of illegal murder or homicide or other major felonies can include but is not limited to pre-meditation, purposefulness, anger, rage, ill-will, or vengeance. Consider the contemporary murder statute that weighs and evaluates these various intents and motivations.

(a) In this section:
    (1) "Adequate cause" means cause that would commonly produce a degree of anger, rage, resentment, or terror in a person of ordinary temper, sufficient to render the mind incapable of cool reflection.
    (2) "Sudden passion" means passion directly caused by and arising out of provocation by the individual killed or another acting with the person killed which passion arises at the time of the offense and is not solely the result of former provocation.

(b) A person commits an offense if he:
    (1) intentionally or knowingly causes the death of an individual;
    (2) intends to cause serious bodily injury and commits an act clearly dangerous to human life that causes the death of an individual; or
    (3) commits or attempts to commit a felony, other than manslaughter, and in the course of and in furtherance of the commission or attempt, or in immediate flight from the commission or attempt, he commits or attempts to commit an act clearly dangerous to human life that causes the death of an individual.

(c) Except as provided by Subsection (d), an offense under this section is a felony of the first degree.

(d) At the punishment stage of a trial, the defendant may raise the issue as to whether he caused the death under the immediate influence of sudden passion arising from an adequate cause. If the defendant proves the issue in the affirmative by a preponderance of the evidence, the offense is a felony of the second degree.[10]

Jesus references murder in the context of emotional anger which can become so consuming that He urges all to soften and assuage the influence of unchecked anger. For Jesus, unbridled anger and rage inevitably lead to other things, including murder. Jesus poignantly proves this point in the Gospel of Matthew.

> But I say to you that if you are angry with a brother or sister, you will be liable to judgment; and if you insult a brother or sister, you will be liable to the council; and if you say, "You fool," you will be liable to the hell of fire. So when you are offering your gift at the altar, if you remember that your brother or sister has something against you, leave your gift there before the altar and go; first be reconciled to your brother or sister and then come and offer your gift. Come to terms quickly with your accuser while you are on the way to court with him, or your accuser may hand you over to the judge, and the judge to the guard, and you will be thrown into prison.[11]

In place of anger and rage, disagreement and strife, find a path to peace and justice; yearn for reconciliation and forgiveness over seeking the eye for an eye. Jesus offers another way of handling harm and victimization, namely that rather than allowing anger to build and plotting vengeance, the injured forgive others who persecute him and, even as hard to hard as it to understand, "turn the other cheek." To be certain, it is a formula that defuses and makes melt away the anger and anguish that often lead to violent conduct. Jesus says:

You have heard that it was said, "An eye for an eye and a tooth for a tooth." But I say to you, Do not resist an evildoer. But if anyone strikes you on the right cheek, turn the other also; and if anyone wants to sue you and take your coat, give your cloak as well; and if anyone forces you to go one mile, go also the second mile. Give to everyone who begs from you, and do not refuse anyone who wants to borrow from you.[12]

Commentary on these passages has been regular and fraught with diverse opinions.[13]

Some argue the passage implies limitless pacifism at the expense of our own lives, others that in minor matters it is not worth a reaction or response if the harm less lethal, and then others conclude that the passage does not apply to more sinister activity like murder. For our natural law makeup, those precepts embedded in our own reason and mind, is naturally more attuned to self-preservation and self-defense than willing death. Suffice it to say, Jesus is making a point with some exaggeration in order that people consider the alternatives to violence with violence in reaction.[14]

Another criterion of intentionality or criminal purpose is the criminal's overall mentality as influenced by his or her surrounding circumstances. Jesus is well aware that crimes often emerge from contagion, mass induced frenzies, and high levels of riot and control. Most insightfully, Jesus recognizes that criminality begets criminality, such as the unleashed or unchecked crowd that grows in a reactionary way. When Moses came down the mountaintop with the Ten Commandments, he witnessed a frenzy, an orgy of sin and idolatry. When God leveled Sodom and Gomorrah, He simply found just a few worthy citizens remaining and spared them—the rest were destroyed, for these citizens had lost their moral bearings, and the more they imbibed sin, the more arrogant and criminally malevolent they become. In other words, one crime leads to another and another; and before one realizes it, everything is tolerated and most acceptable. In our present sphere, one could argue that because abortion has been practiced with such rapidity and lack of thought, some now argue the legitimacy and even utility of infanticide. In this way, people become hardened and even coarser than we could have ever imagined in other times.

One other category of criminal activity signifies this widespread lawlessness, looting, and public disorder, namely, public strife. Strife is defined in many ways, none more commonly as violent public disorder, where the citizenry is running amuck. St. Paul's Letter to the Romans captures strife brilliantly when he states:

> They have become filled with every kind of wickedness, evil, greed and depravity. They are full of envy, murder, strife, deceit and malice. They are gossips, slanderers, God-haters, insolent, arrogant and boastful; they invent ways of doing evil; they disobey their parents; they are senseless, faithless, heartless, ruthless. Although they know God's righteous decree that those who do such things deserve death, they not only continue to do these very things but also approve of those who practice them.[15]

Within this sort of environment, a plethora of crimes, including assault and other bodily injury, is readily discernable. And Jesus sees this just as keenly when He remarks in the Gospel of Luke:

> Be on guard so that your hearts are not weighed down with dissipation and drunkenness and the worries of this life, and that day does not catch you unexpectedly, like a trap. For it will come upon all who live on the face of the whole earth.[16]

Crimes Against the Body

Murder represents the most egregious offense against the body and is rightfully designated the most serious of criminal felonies. Interestingly, Jesus often spoke of lower-level bodily injuries—many of which He personally and most intimately experienced. The Passion of Christ encompasses a wide swath of assault, battery, mutilation, and enhanced forms of torture and punishment. The crowning with thorns, the flogging, the nails driven into the hands, and the spear into the side all represent assaults, most of which would be designated "aggravated" against His entire body.

Consider the state of Maine's Aggravated Assault provision and trans-impose the Passion of Christ.

§208. Aggravated assault
1. A person is guilty of aggravated assault if that person intentionally, knowingly, or recklessly causes:
   A. Bodily injury to another that creates a substantial risk of death or extended convalescence necessary for recovery of physical health. Violation of this paragraph is a Class B crime; [PL 2015, c. 358, §1 (AMD).]
   A-1. Bodily injury to another that causes serious, permanent disfigurement or loss or substantial impairment of the function of any bodily member or organ. Violation of this paragraph is a Class A crime; [PL 2015, c. 358, §1 (NEW).]
   B. Bodily injury to another with use of a dangerous weapon. Violation of this paragraph is a Class B crime; or [PL 2015, c. 358, §1 (AMD).]
   C. Bodily injury to another under circumstances manifesting extreme indifference to the value of human life.[17]

Each provision correlates to the unjustified assault on Jesus by the Roman authorities. Each action taken against Jesus created a "substantial risk" of death—even though these actions, however dastardly and grievous, would be futile exercises to a resurrected Christ. By personal experience, Jesus experienced the agonies common to high level assault cases. Mark's Gospel recognizes this painful reality.

> As for yourselves, beware; for they will hand you over to councils; and you will be beaten in synagogues; and you will stand before governors and kings because of me, as a testimony to them.[18]

Even though He experiences the worst that assault has to offer, His perfection and unceasing charity foretell a kindness we cannot comprehend. While surely not applicable in all cases, and more likely relevant in smaller trifles or disagreements rather than aggravated circumstances, Jesus urges those in fights or assaults to simply "turn the other cheek."

> But I say to you, Do not resist an evildoer. But if anyone strikes you on the right cheek, turn the other also.[19]

In the Gospel of Luke, the recommendation is even more sweeping.

> If anyone strikes you on the cheek, offer the other also; and from anyone who takes away your coat do not withhold even your shirt.[20]

Within these passages, the range of interpretations has been extraordinary in scholarly literature.[21] Some have held that this principle applies in minor assaults and human trifles rather than violent confrontations. Consider how irrational it would be and inconsistent with our base instinct of self-preservation, which is

CHRIST, CRIME, AND MORAL JUDGMENT

rooted in the natural law, to turn the other cheek when attacked by a sledgehammer-wielding assailant. No Christian is obliged to allow self-destruction. On the other hand, in minor scuffles and difficulties, avoiding a pursuit to become evenly placed in responding blow per blow in less than lethal confrontations is more on point for this maxim.[22]

Here Jesus recognizes the world's extensive encounters with fights and arguments, disagreements and getting back at one another. Here it is better to walk away and forgive rather than heap insult upon insult.

In general, Jesus preaches and lives His Gospel of love—love of neighbor and love of God above all else. If we are unable to withstand the natural tensions and frustrations that emerge between neighbors in the temporal sphere, we lack the level of charity necessary for a more virtuous life. Jesus challenges us to look past the insulter, the petty offender, and the assailant lacking the power to cause any serious harm. On the other hand, defense of self, when proportionate and reasonable, is an obligation imposed by self-preservation. In the Garden of Gethsemane, Jesus goes even further in calling on His defenders to lay down the instruments of war they took up in His defense. Matthew recounts:

> Suddenly, one of those with Jesus put his hand on his sword, drew it, and struck the slave of the high priest, cutting off his ear. Then Jesus said to him, "Put your sword back into its place; for all who take the sword will perish by the sword. Do you think that I cannot appeal to my Father, and he will at once send me more than twelve legions of angels?"[23]

When dealing with assault and other bodily injuries, the experiential record of Jesus Christ is unrivaled. Jesus, who suffered at levels hard to fully catalogue, is accurately aware of what it means to be assaulted; for His Passion, death, and resurrection perfectly manifest the aligned suffering these crimes cause. But when offenses occur at the lower tier of gravity and seriousness, Christ lays out a unique and even courageous response: to forgive, to not react or over-react, and to weigh the severity of assault before taking reciprocal action. For Jesus, it is very courageous to take a nonlethal hit and pray for the offender and wait until a more appropriate time to respond. Jesus is a model of charity and compassion, even for those He knows will potentially harm Him. When He asks, in the Gospel of Luke, as He hangs near death on the Cross, for His "Father to forgive them, for they know not what they do," He proves His Divinity; for who else amongst us could achieve this level of forgiveness? The passage in Luke is compelling:

> One of the criminals hanging there taunted Jesus, saying, "Are you not the Christ? Save yourself and us!" But the other rebuked him, "Have you no fear of God, since you are under the same sentence? In our case, we have been condemned justly, for we are getting what we deserve for our deeds. But this man has committed no wrong." Then he said, "Jesus, remember me when you come into your kingdom." Jesus said to him, "Amen, I say to you, today you will be with me in Paradise."[24]

Jesus, despite all the slings and arrows, the whips and the nails, the crown of thorns and the pierced rib, still places the law of charity right in the center of things. He remarks,

> You have heard that it was said, "You shall love your neighbor and hate your enemy." But I say to you, Love your enemies and pray for those who persecute you, so that you may be children of your Father in heaven; for

he makes his sun rise on the evil and on the good, and sends rain on the righteous and on the unrighteous. For if you love those who love you, what reward do you have? Do not even the tax collectors do the same? And if you greet only your brothers and sisters, what more are you doing than others? Do not even the Gentiles do the same? Be perfect, therefore, as your heavenly Father is perfect.[25]

Conclusion

Jesus's analysis of bodily crimes provides a strong undergirding for Western jurisprudence—and in various ways. First, Jesus calls for proof of both the act and the motive and assumes that not all killing is a crime. He is aware of killing in self-defense, times of war, and other exceptions to the charge. Second, the killing alone does not meet the evidentiary standard because Jesus wants proof of the mind, the mens rea—that component that comes from within that triggers the act. Hence, Christ's analysis of murder reflects the two fundamental elements of the offense, namely the act and the mind.

His examples of this sort of evil intent were dangerously reserved to and related to religious leaders, who He claims engaged in murder. Most readers of this commentary see how deeply moved Jesus was in the matter of John the Baptist.

At the same time, Jesus relays a strong correlation of high emotionalism and the rates of murder, manslaughter, and other bodily injury. Part of the reason He continually advises that parties not be consumed by strife and other contagion is because an after effect of this is often violence. Jesus also advises that contentious parties find a path to peace—a way to defuse situations rather than allowing the situation to foster greater physical harm. Many murders and assaults could be avoided if people would work to temper the situation. To "turn the other cheek" is a request to be discretionary—to react in peace and justice when the stakes are not worth further bodily injury.

Finally, the chapter shows how Jesus personally experienced these types of offenses, namely murder, aggravated assault, and bodily mutilation, during His arrest, confinement, crucifixion, and death.

Chapter 4 Endnotes

1 See: "Jesus the Prisoner," Prison Fellowship International, (2024) https://pfi.org/engage/jesus-the-prisoner.
2 Mk 10:17–19 (NRSVCE).
3 Lk 18:18–20 (NRSVCE).
4 Mt 19:18 (NCB); see Mt 19:16–19 also.
5 Mt 5:21–22 (NRSVCE).
6 Mt 23:29–34 (NRSVCE).
7 Charles P. Nemeth, *Criminal Law*, 3rd ed. (Routledge, 2022).
8 Mk 7:20–23 (NRSVCE).
9 Mt 15:19–20 (NRSVCE).
10 Tex. Penal Code § 19.02.
11 Mt 5:22–25 (NRSVCE).
12 Mt 5:38–42 (NRSVCE).
13 Tim Staples, "Turn the Other Cheek," *Catholic Answers*, August 8, 2014, https://www.catholic.com/magazine/online-edition/turn-the-other-cheek.
14 See: Ashley Hooker, "'Turning the Other Cheek'—Bible Meaning and Misunderstandings," Christianity.com, October 10, 2023, https://www.christianity.com/wiki/christian-terms/what-christians-get-wrong-about-turn-the-other-cheek.html.
15 Rom 1:29–32 (NIV).
16 Lk 21:34–35 (NRSVCE).
17 Me. Stat. Title 17-A, §208 (2024).
18 Mk 13:9 (NRSVCE).
19 Mt 5:39 (NRSVCE).
20 Lk 6:29 (NRSVCE).

21 See: Karlo Broussard, "Self Defense and Turning the Other Cheek," *Catholic Answers*, February 16, 2023, https://www.catholic.com/audio/scw/year-a-seventh-sunday-of-ordinary-time.

22 James Martin, "Is Turning the Other Cheek Even Possible?" *America Magazine*, February 19, 2011, https://www.americamagazine.org/content/all-things/turning-other-cheek-even-possible?

23 Mt 26:51–53 (NRSVCE).

24 Lk 23:39–43 (NCB).

25 Mt 5:43-48 (NRSVCE).

Chapter 5: Christ, Crime, and Sexual Offenses

Introduction

In the area of sexual offenses, Christ's commentary is not as comprehensive compared to the pages of the Old Testament, which are replete with references to rape, incest, bestiality, and a host of other sexual infractions. Jesus's coverage of the questions of sexual crimes involves far more nuance.[1] On the other hand, the New Testament is filled with Pauline commentary which hits especially hard on sexual depravity. St. Paul's Letter to the Romans is particularly biting, in which he states:

> Therefore, God gave them up in the lusts of their hearts to impurity, to the degrading of their bodies among themselves, because they exchanged the truth about God for a lie and worshiped and served the creature rather than the Creator, who is blessed forever! Amen.
>
> For this reason, God gave them up to degrading passions. Their women exchanged natural intercourse for unnatural, and in the same way also the men, giving up natural intercourse with women, were consumed with passion for one another. Men committed shameless acts with men and received in their own persons the due penalty for their error.[2]

So much is bound up in this passage: the rage and irrationality of lust and the violations evident in the natural law as the law of nature itself coupled with a denial of the Creator. While St. Paul never hesitates to define and delineate sexual offenses, Christ's approach is reaffirmation of the Decalogue, which contains restrictions on sexual conduct and an unbridled and untethered sexuality without parameters. Christ's commentaries can be explicitly specific, such as in the case of abuse of children, and, at other times, woven into the state of the world with frequent insights into licentiousness, lust, and other outward signs and manifestations of sexual disorder.

Add to this Christ's conclusions on matters involving adultery and fornication, acts long criminalized in Western culture, which did not treat these matters as insignificant but as serious offenses against God and the common good. Within this moral vision, Christ is considered the model of perfect temperance and forgiveness, especially toward all in power. A powerful illustration of this approach was evident in those who challenged Him regarding the adulteress who washed His feet. Jesus told those who critiqued Him:

> "Therefore, I tell you, her sins, which were many, have been forgiven; hence she has shown great love. But the one to whom little is forgiven, loves little." Then he said to her, "Your sins are forgiven." But those who were at the table with him began to say among themselves, "Who is this who even forgives sins?" And he said to the woman, "Your faith has saved you; go in peace."[3]

In this passage, Jesus does not disregard the errant ways of this woman regarding illicit sexual behavior, such as prostitution and promiscuity. Jesus also labels the background of the woman at the well as containing "many sins." Although He forgives these sins, it is on the condition of belief and an abiding and meaningful faith.

Jesus's forgiveness is not without conditions or suggestions for how to live better and more adequately.

Christ's evaluation of sexual depravity is often tied to the vice of lust, for, in the final analysis, sexual offenses reflect not only criminal intentionality but errant behavior that has been habitually formed. In the same way that the chaste person has prized his or her sexual integrity and goodness, the sexual offender engenders sexual dysfunction and harm by continuous acts of lust. In this setting, Christ's psychological insights are extraordinary when He tells His followers:

> If your hand causes you to sin, cut it off. It is preferable for you to enter life maimed than to have two hands and go into the unquenchable fire of Gehenna where the devouring worm never dies and the fire is never quenched. And if your foot causes you to sin, cut it off. It is better for you to enter life crippled than to have two feet and be thrown into Gehenna where the devouring worm never dies and the fire is never quenched. And if your eye causes you to sin, tear it out. It is preferable for you to enter into the kingdom of God with one eye than to have two eyes and be cast into Gehenna, where the devouring worm never dies and the fire is never quenched.[4]

Undeniably, this admonition unequivocally proclaims the necessity of a life of purity and chastity over a life of vice and lust. This psychological approach often plays out in His assessment of human action. St. Paul's various commentaries frequently reflect how sin, especially lust, consumes rationality and makes us into a person faithless person who acts who acts without much reflection. Put another way, sin subsumes and overwhelms our better self. In Romans, St. Paul declares:

For we know that the law is spiritual; but I am of the flesh, sold into slavery under sin. I do not understand my own actions. For I do not do what I want, but I do the very thing I hate. Now if I do what I do not want, I agree that the law is good. But in fact, it is no longer I that do it, but sin that dwells within me. For I know that nothing good dwells within me, that is, in my flesh. I can will what is right, but I cannot do it.[5]

Most of the categories of sexual crime and the corresponding offenses not only enslave and degrade us but throw logic out the window. In agreement with this passage, sexual offenders readily agree that their conduct is wrong, that the depraved mind is not the thinking mind but a body under siege, and that by repetition of sin and its constant control our sense of freedom of choice is lost. It is a deep insight about the power of sexual depravity on the human actor—that same actor identifying the wrong conduct and the aligned sin yet feeling powerless to change. To illustrate, those who professionally work with pedophiles shall easily see the wisdom of St. Paul and the psychological complexity of this offense, for it is not I who acts but the flesh which decides.[6]

Licentiousness and Lewd and Lascivious Behavior

During the time of Christ, pagan morality and a corresponding array of liberal sexual mores were common to the culture. From concubines to legal mistresses to the legalization of brothels and prostitution, at the time of Jesus, the Roman world tolerated behaviors that can be correctly described as licentious.[7]

By contrast, for most of the American experience, from the colonies until the late twentieth century, unseemly, seedy public behavior, especially where and when sexuality was involved, was frowned upon. The last thirty to forty years have seen enormous pressures to liberalize society and even normalize once unacceptable behaviors. California, by way of example, has loosened loitering laws that were often applied to prostitutes roaming the streets in search of business, and the impact on accelerating rates of prostitution has been clear to the state's residents.[8] From the academic world, there are unceasing calls to eliminate long-standing prohibitions of sexual offense, under the guise of protecting women.[9] From the radical feminist perspective, economic arguments as to "making a living" in a life of prostitution are posed without hesitation. Despite these errant movements, most states still proscribe lewd and lascivious behavior. Minnesota still retains a statutory framework which issues a strong condemnation of these unacceptable behaviors.

Subdivision 1. **Misdemeanor.**
A person who commits any of the following acts in any public place, or in any place where others are present, is guilty of a misdemeanor:
(1) willfully and lewdly exposes the person's body, or the private parts thereof;
(2) procures another to expose private parts; or
(3) engages in any open or gross lewdness or lascivious behavior, or any public indecency other than behavior specified in this subdivision.
Subdivision 2. **Gross misdemeanor.**
A person who commits any of the following acts is guilty of a gross misdemeanor:
(1) the person violates subdivision 1 in the presence of a minor under the age of 16; or
(2) the person violates subdivision 1 after having been previously convicted of violating subdivision 1, sections 609.342 to 609.3451, or a statute from another state in conformity with any of those sections.[10]

The statute is broad enough to include diverse forms of lewd and lascivious conduct; at the same time, this statute encompasses the concept of licentiousness. In licentiousness, we discover those who have given themselves up to vice and its control, who have become hardened to the coarseness and inappropriateness of their behavior. In St. Paul's Letter to the Ephesians, he perfectly summarizes this state of impurity:

> They are darkened in their understanding and alienated from the life of God because of their ignorance and their hardness of heart. Having lost all sensitivity, they have abandoned themselves to vice, committing every kind of impurity in growing excess.
> That is not how you learned Christ.[11]

That Jesus understood this moral state is undeniable. In the Gospel of Luke, He contrasts the life of "light" with the licentious state of "darkness."

> Your eye is the lamp of your body. If your eye is healthy, your whole body is full of light; but if it is not healthy, your body is full of darkness. Therefore, consider whether the light in you is not darkness. If then your whole body is full of light, with no part of it in darkness, it will be as full of light as when a lamp gives you light with its rays.[12]

The licentious state may commence with poor habits and undesirable behavior, although Jesus concludes that it is the doorway to more dastardly conduct. Being licentious becomes an almost insufferable condition that impacts our lives day to day. It is an undisciplined and unrestrained existence where the human actor lives in "reveling and drunkenness, … debauchery and licentiousness, …

quarrelling and jealousy."[13] Jesus directly instructs His followers to control themselves and to conduct a serious self-assessment and avoid the negative behaviors that lead to self-destruction.[14] In the Gospel of Luke, Jesus declares:

> Be on guard so that your hearts are not weighed down with dissipation and drunkenness and the worries of this life, and that day does not catch you unexpectedly, like a trap. For it will come upon all who live on the face of the whole earth.[15]

With Christ's perfect knowledge, He keenly calls the licentious life a "trap"; for before one knows it, the lifestyle becomes normalized, even when the intellect and reason know how destructive this behavior is. Jesus calls this way of life a "dissipation"—a sort of devolution in morals and proper living. The licentious lifestyle dissolves the natural and normal barriers needed for a virtuous and productive life. Otherwise, as St. Paul relays, if we live in the flesh, "our sinful passions" will "bear fruit for death."[16]

Adultery

One of the natural offshoots of licentiousness and lewd and lascivious behavior is the many negative impacts of it felt on individuals and the community at large. As moral strictures break down, the aligned institutions crumble as well, such as marriage, the nuclear family, and the care of children.

For most of Western tradition, the idea of adultery was treated as a spiritual, social, and cultural problem; yet at the same time, some jurisdictions codified the act of adultery as a crime. Even today, the liberal state of New York retains the codification.

A person is guilty of adultery when he engages in sexual intercourse
with another person at a time when he has a living spouse, or
the other person has a living spouse.
Adultery is a class B misdemeanor.[17]

At the same time, "adultery" is part of the Decalogue—one of
God's primary proscriptions in human operations. It is neither in-
cidental nor peripheral in the grand scheme of things but central
to God's commands. Like other crimes and errors delineated by
Jesus, adultery ranks as an equal to theft, wickedness, and deceit.
In the Gospel of Mark, Jesus states:

> What comes out of a man is what defiles a man. For from
> within, out of the heart of man, come evil thoughts, for-
> nication, theft, murder, adultery, coveting, wickedness, de-
> ceit, licentiousness, envy, slander, pride, foolishness. All
> these evil things come from within, and they defile a man.[18]

Jesus goes even further in His condemnation of adultery as
both act and simple intention. Put another way, the adulterous
party commits the act by either thought or actual deed—a curious
if not unique construction for any crime. Surely, adultery, under
ordinary circumstances, calls for the affirmative act of sexual relations with a married party, or in the context of a bigamous or
polygamous relationship, or as a predictable offshoot of fornication. Jesus takes adultery to an even higher continuum of action
by stressing the mental state of the offending party. In other words,
Jesus declares that adultery can and is the result of lustful intentionality. The Gospel of Matthew lays out this unique perspective:

> But I say to you that everyone who looks at a woman
> with lust has already committed adultery with her in
> his heart.[19]

Hence, in Christ's view, adultery is both an internal and external act.

Coupled with adultery, as a natural consequence or collateral harm, is the act of divorce which leads to the dissolution of marriage. As in other locations in the New Testament, Jesus never hesitates to list those actions which preclude the heavenly afterlife. Not surprisingly, murder is always on the list but at the same time, so too adultery. Jesus reiterates over and over: "You know the commandments: 'Do not commit adultery, Do not kill, Do not steal, Do not bear false witness, Honor your father and mother.'"[20]

That Jesus expends so much energy on the crime of adultery gives testimony to its seriousness rather than its current triviality. It is fair to argue that adultery, just as fornication, opens a door to other sexual errors. As Jesus indicates, divorce leads to adultery; and as adultery becomes more repetitive in the story of the woman with five former marriages, we do not lose the picture of wayward families, neglected spouses, illegitimate births, and abandoned children. In short, adultery, as well as fornication, has a domino effect. As if this be not enough, Jesus deals with adultery at two other settings.

The Woman at the Well

In the first of two stories concerning adultery, Jesus encounters a divorced woman—a state of life He neither tolerates nor accepts. For Jesus perceived divorce as a force which further fractures marriage and the family. When Jesus converses with a woman, He asks her to call for her husband, to which she replies:

> "I have no husband." Jesus said to her, "You are right in saying, 'I have no husband'; for you have had five husbands, and the one you have now is not your husband. What you have said is true!"[21]

See Figure 7

Christ and the Samaritan Woman at the Well by Jacob van Oost the Younger, 1668

From Jesus's perspective, a woman or man with five spouses has already gone down the road of adultery, for in Christ's view marrying divorced parties or marrying or consorting with other married partners or having sexual relations with others while a spouse is still alive constitutes two offenses, namely adultery and divorce. Despite this checkered past, Jesus is gracious and forgiving. At the same time, Jesus reacts to her hopes and longings for the Messiah, to which He replied,

> "But the hour is coming, and is now here, when the true worshipers will worship the Father in spirit and truth, for the Father seeks such as these to worship him. God is spirit, and those who worship him must worship in spirit and truth." The woman said to him, "I know that Messiah is coming" (who is called Christ). "When he comes, he will proclaim all things to us." Jesus said to her, "I am he, the one who is speaking to you."[22]

At various times bystanders, His own disciples, and the Pharisees seemed troubled by Jesus associating with those considered "less than"—and indicated that the penalty for this behavior was stoning. Jesus in no way obliged and, in fact, objected to this tactic, explaining:

> Let anyone among you who is without sin be the first
> to throw a stone at her.[23]

In this curious story, Jesus lays out an alternative path and remedy other than the radical one of stoning. Instead of stoning and death, why not convert and save the woman at the well? The beauty and brilliance of Jesus's approach to sin rests in stark contrast to the Pharisaical approach or justice system which merely depends on legal definitions and processes. Jesus Christ offers a new way of life for those who seek Him.

See Figure 8.

Mary Magdalene: Casting out Demons and Washing the Feet of Jesus

A famous and recurring figure in the New Testament, Mary Magdalene, represents the second story of adultery, fornication, and even alleged prostitution and its correlation to sin and redemption. Questions regarding the accuracy of these claims about Mary Magdalene are centuries old.[24] While most biblical scholars agree that "seven demons" were cast out of her, precisely what those demons were is not explicitly noted in the Bible. In Luke, we read about "some women who had been cured of evil spirits and infirmities: Mary, called Magdalene, from whom seven demons had gone out."[25]

Not in dispute is that upon meeting Jesus, Mary Magdalene experienced a profound directional change in her life—all of which is attributable to Jesus.[26] For it was Mary Magdalene to whom Christ first appeared after the Resurrection; it was Mary Magdalene who first visited the tomb having come to anoint Jesus, and to whom the Angel announced the Resurrected Jesus. And others have made the claim that it was Mary Magdalene, though a sinner, who visited Jesus and washed His feet with her tears. Whether the story can be verified is unclear, but what the Gospels indicate is that a washing had taken place. Below is the partial story from the Gospel of Luke.

> One of the Pharisees asked him to eat with him, and he went into the Pharisee's house, and sat at table. And behold, a woman of the city, who was a sinner, when she learned that he was reclining at table in the Pharisee's house, brought an alabaster flask of ointment, and standing behind him at his feet, weeping, she began to wet his feet with her tears, and wiped them with the hair of her head, and kissed his feet, and anointed them with the ointment. Now when the Pharisee who had invited him saw it, he said to himself, "If this man

were a prophet, he would have known who and what sort of woman this is who is touching him, for she is a sinner." …

Then turning toward the woman he said to Simon, "Do you see this woman? I entered your house, you gave me no water for my feet, but she has wet my feet with her tears and wiped them with her hair. You gave me no kiss, but from the time I came in she has not ceased to kiss my feet. You did not anoint my head with oil, but she has anointed my feet with ointment."[27]

Those around Jesus, His followers and disciples, and those in the Pharisaical sect, wondered out loud how Jesus could have stooped so low as to associate with a sinner of this caliber—and whether it is Mary Magdalene or not can never be completely resolved. Even though the historical accuracy is lacking, the story behind it illustrates the magnanimity of Jesus and His boundless generosity. As the conversation continued, Jesus tells those near that I understand she is a sinner, I accept that reality, but, given her acts of honor and respect, it is I that shall forgive. In one of the New Testament's most beautiful passages, Jesus gives peace and solace to a sinner—one likely plagued by the sexual offenses Jesus gave witness to.

"Therefore, I tell you, her sins, which were many, have been forgiven; hence she has shown great love. But the one to whom little is forgiven, loves little." Then he said to her, "Your sins are forgiven." But those who were at the table with him began to say among themselves, "Who is this who even forgives sins?" And he said to the woman, "Your faith has saved you; go in peace."[28]

Sodomy and Homosexuality

While both the Old and New Testaments expressly provide support for the prohibition of homosexuality, Christ never directly tackles the subject matter.[29] By Him not mentioning it, one should not impute consent, nor would it be fair to insist that the silence of Jesus was intentional. Nor can it be deduced that silence on the subject is consent, especially when one considers how uncommon this conversation would have been 2000 years ago. Sexual orientation was simply not on the average person's radar. To be sure, Christ covers many, many crimes, but surely not all of them. One could also conclude that Jesus's examination of licentiousness or lewd and lascivious behavior might encompass these acts.

Though express declarations by Jesus may be in short supply, the two Testaments are replete with commentary from both prophets and disciples. And for most centuries in Western jurisprudence, nearly twenty to be exact, the question of homosexuality and sodomy was indisputably condemned by design. In *Bowers v. Hardwick*,[30] the U. S. Supreme Court affirmed the right of states to criminalize the activity—and that was in 1985. Shockingly, the Court overruled its precedent in *Lawrence v. Texas*[31] in 2014, thus opening the floodgates of sexual inventiveness rooted in alleged rights. No greater critic of these practices exists than St. Paul. In his Letter to the Romans, St. Paul declares that these practices are derived from lust and all manner of impurity.

> Therefore, God gave them up in the lusts of their hearts to impurity, to the degrading of their bodies among themselves, because they exchanged the truth about God for a lie and worshiped and served the creature rather than the Creator, who is blessed forever! Amen.[32]

St. Paul's description of homosexuality could not be factually plainer and features both male and female versions of homosexuality. In addition, the acts are termed "shameless" and "unnatural" as well as "consumed with passion." These descriptors are not, by any measure, favorable.

> For this reason, God gave them up to degrading passions. Their women exchanged natural intercourse for unnatural, and in the same way also the men, giving up natural intercourse with women, were consumed with passion for one another. Men committed shameless acts with men and received in their own persons the due penalty for their error.[33]

The critique is intense and without apology, and the sexual immorality described is symptomatic of other negative traits and disobedience to the laws of nature and the laws of God. St. Paul refers to these actors as debased and filled with malice, rebellious, and ruthlessness. This passage paints a grotesque picture of complete defiance and unacceptability.

> And since they did not see fit to acknowledge God, God gave them up to a debased mind and to things that should not be done. They were filled with every kind of wickedness, evil, covetousness, malice. Full of envy, murder, strife, deceit, craftiness, they are gossips, slanderers, God-haters, insolent, haughty, boastful, inventors of evil, rebellious toward parents, foolish, faithless, heartless, ruthless. They know God's decree, that those who practice such things deserve to die—yet they not only do them but even applaud others who practice them.[34]

All of these traits manifest misplaced priorities before God and man, or as the Letter to the Romans indicates, those engaged in these practices represent a "mind that is set on the flesh" and "is hostile to God."[35]

The Special Case of Pedophilia

That Jesus had a special place in His heart for small children cannot be argued. Urging His followers to allow children to come close was a common request for Him. In the Gospel of Mark, He thwarts efforts by His disciples to keep children away so they would not be a nuisance, because, in fact, Christ wanted them by His side.

> People were bringing little children to him in order that he might touch them; and the disciples spoke sternly to them. But when Jesus saw this, he was indignant and said to them, "Let the little children come to me; do not stop them; for it is to such as these that the kingdom of God belongs. Truly I tell you, whoever does not receive the kingdom of God as a little child will never enter it." And he took them up in his arms, laid his hands on them, and blessed them.[36]

Christ beckons the children to come near and always for the same reason—their innocence and goodness and the fact that the world has the power to corrupt them. To harm children, in any way or fashion, is an act of vile proportions. Most American jurisdictions share this outrage. See the state of Nebraska's law on child sexual abuse.

28-319.01. Sexual assault of a child; first degree; penalty.
(1) A person commits sexual assault of a child in the first degree:

(a) When he or she subjects another person under twelve years of age to sexual penetration and the actor is at least nineteen years of age or older; or

(b) When he or she subjects another person who is at least twelve years of age but less than sixteen years of age to sexual penetration and the actor is twenty-five years of age or older.

(2) Sexual assault of a child in the first degree is a Class IB felony with a mandatory minimum sentence of fifteen years in prison for the first offense.[37]

In Jesus, we witness an intense love of children, coupled with a protectionist mentality that always seeks to maintain their innocence. The scandals of clerics and bishops, even though they are a select lot over the last fifty years, are the sorts of harm and injury that Christ cannot and will not tolerate. The clerical authorities do not always share the Savior's intense desire to protect children; and, much to the chagrin of the faithful, there have been far too many scandals and coverups in the Church at large.[38] So outraged is Jesus when considering the issue of children being abused, physically or sexually, that His penalty is terminal. It is the sort of criminal act that deserves the ultimate punishment. Jesus declares:

> If anyone causes one of these little ones who believe in me to sin, it would be better for him if a great millstone were hung around his neck and he were thrown into the sea.[39]

In Matthew's Gospel, the severity of Christ's judgment and His reaction to the harm or abuse of children is even more draconian.

> But if anyone causes one of these little ones who believe in me to sin, it would be better for him to have a

millstone fastened around his neck and to be drowned in the depths of the sea.[40]

The outrage is properly proportionate and strong evidence that Jesus is an unrivaled figure in the history of moral judgment. With the case of little children, He displays no hesitation or timidity and instead manifests a fierce call for justice—to the point of death.

Conclusion

Jesus's coverage of sexual crimes comprises an interesting mix of vice, sin, and human failure. As in other forms of crime, Jesus makes plain that the provisions of the Old Testament are still relevant and integrated into His overall philosophy. Jesus never rejects the content of the Old Testament, and this is very important in the overall understanding of sexual crime and related offenses. In the Old Testament there are noticeable references to homosexuality and sodomy, rape, incest, and bestiality—all crimes less covered in the New Testament. By the omission of them in the Gospels, advocates for certain liberalization of sexual mores use the "silence" as proof that Jesus approved of them. However, this supposition is without justification, for during the time of Jesus, debates on these behaviors did not even exist. Nor must the liberalizer forget the extensive coverage Jesus gives to vices such as "lust" and the multiple references to lewd, debaucherous behavior. On top of this, the chapter refers to the tough and unapologetic condemnations of sodomy and other licentiousness by St. Paul in his Letter to the Romans.

In addition, the Decalogue gives support to the Christian view of sexuality; for Jesus frequently refers to the Sixth Commandment, "Thou Shall Not Commit Adultery," and the Tenth Commandment, "Thou Shall Not Covet Thy Neighbor's Wife." In the matter of adultery, Jesus declares that the mere intention or desire to commit the act is sufficient for condemnation. This quite radical position illustrates the seriousness of sexual activity outside specific parameters like marriage.

Jesus expends a good deal of time covering lustful desires and the cumulative effect of sexual promiscuity, prostitution, and other debaucherous activity. Its repetitive nature tends to rot the human person. Each of these behaviors enslaves the human person and tends to lead to greater sin.

Finally, the abuse of children receives special attention from Jesus Christ. Aside from His fierce condemnation of those who perpetrate acts against children, like the pedophile, Christ's penalty for these hideous acts is death.

Chapter 5 Endnotes

1   See Lam 5:11 (NRSVCE): "Women are raped in Zion, virgins in the towns of Judah."
2   Rom 1:24–27 (NRSVCE)
3   Lk 7: 47–48 (NRSVCE).
4   Mk 9:43–48 (NCB).
5   Rom 7:14–18 (NRSVCE).
6   No effort is made to excuse the behavior in the least, but instead to discern how pedophilia has inordinate influence over actors who can rationally see the wrong in the conduct chosen. See: James Keet McElhaney, "Pedophilia: Understanding the Origins and Problems within the Criminal Justice System," (PhD diss., Liberty University, 2023), https://digitalcommons.liberty.edu/cgi/viewcontent.cgi?article=5865&context=doctoral.
7   See: Thomas A. J. McGinn, *Prostitution, Sexuality, and the Law in Ancient Rome*, 2nd ed. (Oxford University Press, 2003).
8   See: California Family Council, "Decriminalizing Prostitution Makes Communities Unsafe," January 18, 2023, https://www.californiafamily.org/2023/01/decriminalizing-prostitution-makes-communities-unsafe.
9   "To Protect Women, Legalize Prostitution," *Harvard Civil Rights-Civil Liberties Law Review*, https://journals.law.harvard.edu/crcl/to-protect-women-legalize-prostitution.

10 Minn. Stat. §617.23 (2024).

11 Eph 4:18–20 (NCB).

12 Lk 11:34–36 (NRSVCE).

13 Rom 13:13 (RSVCE).

14 See: April R. Haynes, "'Licentiousness in All Its Forms,' In Riotous Flesh," (University of Chicago Press, 2015), https://doi.org/10.7208/chicago/9780226284767.003.0003.

15 Lk 21:34–35 (NRSVCE).

16 Rom 7:5 (NRSVCE).

17 N.Y. Penal Law § 255.17 (2024); See also: Dave McKinley, "Bill Seeks to Decriminalize Adultery Across New York State," WGRZ.com, March 22, 2024, https://www.wgrz.com/article/news/crime/bill-seeks-to-decriminalize-adultery-new-york-state/71-4cfeb792-9e45-43b9-bc59-2008d9e834a0.

18 Mk 7:20–23 (RSVCE).

19 Mt 5:28–29 (NRSVCE).

20 Lk 18:20 (RSVCE).

21 Jn 4:17–18 (NRSVCE).

22 Jn 4:23–26 (NRSVCE).

23 Jn 8:7 (NRSVCE).

24 Heidi Schlumpf, guest, *Glad You Asked*, podcast, episode, "Was Mary Magdalene a Prostitute?" U.S. Catholic, April 5, 2024,, https://uscatholic.org/articles/202404/glad-you-asked-was-mary-magdalene-a-prostitute.

25 Lk 8:2 (NRSVCE).

26 See: James Carroll, "Who Was Mary Magdalene?" *Ask Smithsonian*, June 2006, https://www.smithsonianmag.com/history/who-was-mary-magdalene-119565482.

27 Lk 7:36–39, 44–46 (RSVCE).

28 Lk 7:47–50 (NRSVCE).

29 Charles Grondin, "Why Jesus Never Talked About Homosexuality," *Catholic Answers*, https://www.catholic.com/qa/why-jesus-never-talked-about-homosexuality.

30 478 U.S. 186 (1986).

31 539 U.S. 558 (2003).

32 Rom 1:24–25 (NRSVCE).

33 Rom 1:26–27 (NRSVCE).

34 Rom 1:28–32 (NRSVCE).

35 Rom 8:7 (NRSVCE).
36 Mk 10:13–16 (NRSVCE).
37 Neb. Rev. Stat. §28-319.01 (2024).
38 Michael Sean Winters, "US Bishops' Decline into Irrelevance Will Continue," *National Catholic Reporter*, November 17, 2022, https://www.ncronline.org/opinion/ncr-voices/us-bishops-decline-irrelevance-will-continue; see: United States Conference of Catholic Bishops, Charter for the Protection of Children and Young People (2018), https://www.usccb.org/offices/child-and-youth-protection/charter-protection-children-and-young-people.
39 Mk 9:42–49 (NCB).
40 Mt 18:6 (NCB).

Chapter 6: Christ, Crime, and Offenses Against Property

Introduction

In any criminal codification, aside from the natural emphasis given to murder, bodily offenses like assault and battery, and the rightful coverage of sexual offenses which assume many forms, the question of property crimes cannot be overlooked. In fact, Jesus expends significant time and energy discussing questions of property and the rights thereto. It is neither an afterthought nor insignificant addition. The property analysis posed by Jesus covers a great deal of territory. First, one can sensibly deduct that Jesus sees property crime through the lens of private ownership. This sentiment should not be deemed unimportant, for many camps and schools of thought often urge collective ownership as preferable to individual ownership. In fact, Jesus is often labeled "socialistic" since He urges His followers to distribute their private property.[1] This is an incorrect and myopic view of Christ's property system. At no place in the New Testament do we discover the condemnation of private property, although we do encounter stories about ownership, whether it be land or currency. However, the words of Jesus surely and most explicitly condemn the sins of "theft" and "stealing" from another.

> For out of the heart come evil intentions, murder, adultery, fornication, theft, false witness, slander. These are what defile a person, but to eat with unwashed hands does not defile.[2]

Where Jesus dramatically inputs some negativism about the concept of property ownership relates to the lust for it, the influence of greed and envy in property comparisons, and the obsessive compulsion to amass more and more property. A frequent observation made by Jesus is that material goods are not worth a person's soul or the loss of eternal life. Jesus makes repeated references to this reality.

Sell your possessions and give alms. Make purses for yourselves that do not wear out, an unfailing treasure in heaven, where no thief comes near and no moth destroys.[3]

Being compulsively obsessed with property ownership is more the problem in the eyes of Jesus than ownership itself. In Luke, He observes:

> Take care! Be on your guard against all kinds of greed; for one's life does not consist in the abundance of possessions.[4]

Christian tradition has long supported the view that vice-laden possessory interest in property is more the issue than mere ownership. Becoming obsessed with the accumulation of material goods at the costs of a virtuous life precipitates the destruction of one's soul, and Christ continually warns His followers of this result. One of His followers, Zacchaeus, the dreaded tax collector, was quite wealthy, so much so that he was concerned about his ability to earn his eternal reward. Hence, he began to divest himself of his wealth and give to those in need. His exchange with Jesus illuminates the dilemma of unrestrained wealth in the Gospel of Luke:

> But Zacchaeus stood up and said to the Lord, "Look, Lord! Here and now I give half of my possessions to the poor, and if I have cheated anybody out of anything, I will pay back four times the amount."

Jesus said to him, "Today salvation has come to this house, because this man, too, is a son of Abraham. For the Son of Man came to seek and to save the lost."[5]

See Figure 9.

The story of Zacchaeus causes the reader to find a balance between possessions, material goods, money, and a virtuous life and disposition. There is no hard and fast rule but rather a mean, a balance as Aristotle so brilliantly posed, that must be discovered. Aristotelian possessions are neither too much nor too little, but a sensible mean between the two worlds of ownership. This is also true in full-blown economic systems. Many of the world's current conflicts are born of differences in these views—from the social-ist-communist pining for collective ownership and redistribution to the wildly excessive capitalist who has more money than can ever be spent.

In his encyclical letter *Centesimus Annus*, St. John Paul II holds that while capitalism can suffer from a neutral morality—a profit mentality without boundaries—this not a virtuous state of affairs. This lack of boundaries is usually caused by a lust for possessions and excessive greed that is not positively conducive to the moral order unless guided by virtue.[6] To be sure, capitalism represents a greater chance to advance virtue than other systems because it en-courages initiative and self-flourishing and provides incentives, while other systems, like communism, are blatantly discouraging to personal initiative.

While John Paul II lauds free markets as the best amongst all choices, he also warns that capitalism should not and cannot be "unbridled." Despite this shortcoming, when compared to other economic systems, it is still the best and most inherently just sys-tem. Hence, private ownership is to be fully encouraged.[7] Pope Leo XIII authored a brilliant critique of the alternatives, either communism or socialism, and concluded that these systems are antithetical to Catholicism. In *Rerum Novarum*, he holds that so-cialism "*must be utterly rejected*, since it only injures those whom it would seem meant to benefit, is directly contrary to the natural rights of mankind, and would introduce confusion and disorder into the commonweal."[8]

Indeed, it would be difficult to identify success stories in the communist or socialist realm. Surely the old Soviet Union, Cuba, Chad, Angola, and China are not garden spots for freedom and human flourishing. Some of the greatest injustices possible have germinated in Marxism and socialism.

The questions posed here differentiate and distinguish how

economic systems value property and, given the intensity of interest in property, directly correlate to the criminalization of property in a wide array of contexts. For if all is collectively owned, who can commit thievery? On the other hand, if the property is in fact mine to possess and own, then property crime becomes logically enforceable. Even in the American experience, tensions exist as to whether property crimes should always be enforceable. In New York and California, laws have been redrafted to downplay the seriousness of property crime when valuations are between \$950–1150.[9] For Jesus, property offenses are always possible, since they are spurred on by inordinate vices such as greed, envy, lust, and miserliness. The key to understanding Christ's examination of property and its impact, both in a positive or negative way, is to discover the balance and virtuous mean in ownership.

Property Crime and the Decalogue

As is typically the case, the definition and description of crime and criminal activity can be discovered and discerned in the Decalogue. The commandment "Thou shall not Steal" would make little sense in a communist or socialist system since these political designs devalue one's capacity to own and protect property. Since there are only Ten Commandments, being listed as one of the chosen rules for human life signifies the centrality of this admonition. Another commandment pertinently instructs and commands us to forego covetousness in a whole host of affairs, from a neighbor's wife to anything that belongs to a neighbor, even a donkey or an ox. The Tenth Commandment reads:

> You shall not covet your neighbor's house; you shall not covet your neighbor's wife, or male or female slave, or ox, or donkey, or anything that belongs to your neighbor.[10]

Covetousness is this inordinate craving or desire that leads to greed, envy, lust, and the other capital sins. Covetousness leads to shaping and formulating a criminal intentionality to steal.

As in murder and other listed offenses, Jesus indicates that theft and stealing are contrary to any path to eternal life. Obeying the designated commandments is shown as hardly a discretionary option when it's stated:

> As he was setting out on a journey, a man ran up and knelt before him, and asked him, "Good Teacher, what must I do to inherit eternal life?" Jesus said to him, "Why do you call me good? No one is good but God alone. You know the commandments: 'You shall not murder; You shall not commit adultery; You shall not steal; You shall not bear false witness; You shall not defraud; Honor your father and mother.'"[11]

On closer reading, Jesus lays out a very contemporary view of theft and its many forms; for it is not just the traditional larceny of which He speaks, the physical taking of property from another, but also the deceptive and fraudulent method and means to the taking. Nearly side by side with "You shall not steal," Jesus instructs that "You shall not defraud." The language of Christ puts full emphasis on the common understanding of theft, though His purposeful mention of the term "defraud" indicates an awareness that theft and larceny can be far more sinister and complex.

To illustrate, consider the state of Pennsylvania's classic definition of larceny or theft:

§ 3921. Theft by unlawful taking or disposition.
(a) Movable property.—A person is guilty of theft if he unlawfully

takes, or exercises unlawful control over, movable property of another with intent to deprive him thereof.

(b) **Immovable property.**—A person is guilty of theft if he unlawfully transfers, or exercises unlawful control over, immovable property of another or any interest therein with intent to benefit himself or another not entitled thereto.[12]

Compare and contrast Jesus's words with the theft by deception provision, which encompasses His admonition that "You shall not defraud."

§ 3922. Theft by deception.

(a) **Offense defined.**—A person is guilty of theft if he intentionally obtains or withholds property of another by deception. A person deceives if he intentionally:

(1) creates or reinforces a false impression, including false impressions as to law, value, intention, or other state of mind; but deception as to a person's intention to perform a promise shall not be inferred from the fact alone that he did not subsequently perform the promise;

(2) prevents another from acquiring information which would affect his judgment of a transaction; or

(3) fails to correct a false impression which the deceiver previously created or reinforced, or which the deceiver knows to be influencing another to whom he stands in a fiduciary or confidential relationship.[13]

Jesus's own words capture deception in many forms, especially as it relates to the concept of bearing false witness against others. In all the Gospels, Jesus states, "Do not bear false witness."[14] False witness commonly applies to property offenses and is discoverable in forgery and false utterances, document tampering, title fraud, and forgery. In the oral sense, utterances and false statements can lead to property manipulation and theft of all sorts. Today there are so many ways to steal and engage in intentional falsehoods in order to illegally acquire another's property that the code books are running long lists to keep up with the innovations in theft. See Pennsylvania's Table of Theft Crimes by way of example at Figure 10.[15]

Figure 10

Section 3922.1	-	Financial exploitation of an older adult or care-dependent person
Section 3923	-	Theft by extortion
Section 3924	-	Theft of property lost, mislaid, or delivered by mistake
Section 3925	-	Receiving stolen property
Section 3926	-	Theft of services
Section 3927	-	Theft by failure to make required disposition of funds received
Section 3928	-	Unauthorized use of automobiles and other vehicles
Section 3929	-	Retail theft
Section 3929.1	-	Library theft
Section 3929.2	-	Unlawful possession of retail or library theft instruments
Section 3929.3	-	Organized retail theft
Section 3930	-	Theft of trade secrets
Section 3931	-	Theft of unpublished dramas and musical compositions
Section 3932	-	Theft of leased property
Section 3933	-	Unlawful use of computer (Repealed)
Section 3934	-	Theft from a motor vehicle
Section 3935	-	Theft of secondary metal (Unconstitutional)
Section 3935.1	-	Theft of secondary metal
Section 3936	-	Theft of mail

Jesus reminds His followers to be careful about what they say, whether in oral or written form. For all of that is spoken that is false, careless, and malevolent will eventually emerge on the day of judgment. Jesus declares:

> I tell you that on the day of judgment people will have to render an account for every careless word they utter. For by your words you will be justified, and by your words you will be condemned.[16]

As in Jesus's time, the plague of property offenses was a constant challenge of enforcement. Today, the once vaunted clarity of theft being a moral wrong has been muddied in diverse ways, such as the concept of theft as a form of reparations or payback or the notion that since theft is not a violent crime, it should not be high on our justice system's list of priorities. Today, another rationale perversely argues that since the crime happens with such frequency it is better to decriminalize it or reduce its definition to a similar plane as a traffic ticket. Noted already are statutory efforts toward this in California and New York, where stolen property up to a threshold sum can be stolen without much consequence.[17]

In many respects, even though the Decalogue expressly condemns theft, the modern legislative process has so trivialized the act of theft as to make it legal. And the means, methods, and mechanisms to steal are myriad, with so many types and forms of theft it is hard to fully catalog them all. Pennsylvania attempts to list all the fraudulent means of theft as shown above in Figure 10.

Jesus is aware of the impact of theft and banditry on the community at large, and as Shepherd for the flock of humanity, He labels false prophets and imitators of truth as thieves. Reserving this designation for them seems to be a significant critique for those who lead others astray. In the Gospel of John, Jesus stated:

> All who came before me were thieves and bandits; but the sheep did not listen to them. I am the gate. Whoever enters by me will be saved and will come in and go out and find pasture. The thief comes only to steal and kill and destroy. I came that they may have life and have it abundantly.[18]

As Jesus describes the thief—one who comes to steal, kill, and destroy—we encounter a very serious examiner of this crime, who neither downplays its impact on communities nor gives any sympathy for those efforts to decriminalize it.

Other Property Offenses

Throughout the New Testament, Jesus frequently comments on particular criminal offenses; and the range, depth, and breadth of these comments are impressive. Theft, as just witnessed, is a centerpiece and not an afterthought. Theft, Jesus advises, causes havoc in the tranquility of the community and the person harmed by its negative effects. The fact that Jesus separates physical theft from theft by fraud manifest a prophetic glimpse into the new and diversified means to committing theft in our modern culture. There are other offenses that do not escape Jesus's eye.

Robbery

In contrast to theft, robbery is the forcible taking or taking by violent means of the property of another. Jesus's expositions on this designated crime are both challenging and unique. In His description of robbery, we encounter settings most would not anticipate as locales for carrying out this felony. When soldiers approach John the Baptist, as noted in the Gospel of Luke, their natural dominance over the citizenry is evident, and relying on Jesus' teaching, his reply fairly telling:

> Soldiers also asked him, "And we, what should we do?"
> He said to them, "Do not extort money from anyone
> by threats or false accusation, and be satisfied with your
> wages."[19]

Jesus knows and appreciates the darkest damage that arises in war, for throughout recorded history, the theatres of war find soldiers that rape, rob, and pillage. One need only review the latter part of 1945, when the Russian Army retook all of their stolen lands, all the way to the city center of Berlin, and in the process raped and robbed without restraint.[20] The power of the soldier's position turns the thief into something more egregious and dastardlier. When Jesus employs the term "threat" in the taking, He completely captures the essence of robbery—for robbery is the forcible taking of something, not the mere taking. Jesus surely knew how the might and power of the Roman military machine led to many injustices amongst the population. In His own case, the force exerted was almost immeasurable. In robbery, the force or threat can be physical or verbal, though imminently so and delivered with the capacity to inflict serious harm. Any soldier may possess both characteristics—at least the unjust members of the military.

A typical robbery statute, from the state of Kansas, edifies the threat principle:

21-5420. Robbery; aggravated robbery. (a) Robbery is knowingly taking property from the person or presence of another by force or by threat of bodily harm to any person.

(b) Aggravated robbery is robbery, as defined in subsection (a), when committed by a person who:

(1) Is armed with a dangerous weapon; or

(2) inflicts bodily harm upon any person in the course of such robbery.

(c) (1) Robbery is a severity level 5, person felony.

(2) Aggravated robbery is a severity level 3, person felony.[21]

Robbery's definition in Kansas was really its definition at the time of Christ, for the perpetrator either takes by force or by threat of bodily harm.

One other glaring, if not shocking, illustration of the crime of robbery resides in the Jewish Temple. It is an interesting insight into how property can be taken under threat of force or by any particular law or position. Hence, in the Temple, money exchanged for spiritual status or reward became common, in the same way that simony did in the corrupted halls of select Catholic churches where salvation was sold for a shilling. What was going on in the Temple of Jerusalem clearly generated the ire of Jesus Christ because it turned a house of prayer into a "den of robbers." The Gospel of Mark tells the dramatic story:

> Then they came to Jerusalem. And he entered the temple and began to drive out those who were selling and those who were buying in the temple, and he overturned the tables of the money changers and the seats of those who sold doves; and he would not allow anyone to carry anything through the temple. He was teaching and saying, "Is it not written,
> 'My house shall be called a house of prayer for all the nations'? But you have made it a den of robbers."
> And when the chief priests and the scribes heard it, they kept looking for a way to kill him; for they were afraid of him, because the whole crowd was spellbound by his teaching.[22]

In the Gospel of John, the outrage exhibited by Jesus was something rarely if ever witnessed by the disciples. Even as He hung from the Cross, His compassion and the forgiveness He extends can only be described as divine in origin. Contrast the Cross with the Temple, and one encounters a Christ on the attack to drive out the unholiness that has invaded this holiest of places. In John's Gospel, He even uses a whip, turns over the tables, and pours out all the earned coins across the Temple floor. When Christ uses the term "den of robbers," His judgment is fierce and unapologetic. The Gospel declares:

See Figure 11 on the following page.

Jesus Casting Out the Money Changers at the Temple by Carl Heinrich Bloch, 1874

In the temple he found people selling cattle, sheep, and doves, and the money changers seated at their tables. Making a whip of cords, he drove all of them out of the temple, both the sheep and the cattle. He also poured out the coins of the money changers and overturned their tables. He told those who were selling the doves, "Take these things out of here! Stop making my Father's house a marketplace!"[23]

The entire confrontation manifests a Jesus willing to make judgments and to take extraordinary risks in doing so, for Jesus was already on the radar of the Temple authorities. He was no favorite amongst the rabbinical class. Why Jesus chose the word, "robber," rather than "thief" or "embezzler," says much about the intensity of the insult, for the Temple was and is a sacred place, not a shop for pigeon sellers who hold out as holy leaders. Jesus goes even further than the designation of "robber" and heaps the title of extortionist onto the Temple authorities. An extortionist makes threats to get the property he wants. An extortionist operates like a mob figure who communicates every imaginable threat so that you might pay or reward him in some way. At the same time, Jesus jabs the Temple priests and scribes with worrying about the cleanliness of cups and plates rather the goodness in one's heart. In Matthew 23:27, Jesus pulls no punches:

> Woe to you, scribes and Pharisees, hypocrites! For you are like whitewashed tombs, which on the outside look beautiful, but inside they are full of the bones of the dead and of all kinds of filth.[24]

St. Paul piles on the condemnation by listing those precluded from Heaven, and the group includes extortionists: "Thieves, extortioners, drunkards, slanderers, swindlers—none of these will inherit the kingdom of God."[25] In many ways, this combination of authority, like the soldier already noted and the spiritual leader mentioned here, makes the general population feel intimidated and more likely than not to part with their money in order that their souls may be better prepared for the afterlife. The position of religious authority becomes the quiet yet undeniable taking of another's property. It is a subtle threat but a very real one—it is the same threat and ruse which opened the door to sexual abuse in the Catholic Church and, for that matter, literally every Church. Souls and persons are groomed to act in ways they ordinarily would not. In cases where the confessional was utilized to target potential victims, one can capture the parallel.

The *Catechism of the Catholic Church* defines simony in the following way:

> *Simony* is defined as the buying or selling of spiritual things. To Simon the magician, who wanted to buy the spiritual power he saw at work in the apostles, St. Peter responded: "Your silver perish with you, because you thought you could obtain God's gift with money!" Peter thus held to the words of Jesus: "You received without pay, give without pay." It is impossible to appropriate to oneself spiritual goods and behave toward them as their owner or master, for they have their source in God. One can receive them only from him, without payment.[26]

In particular, simony is a fraudulent game, a sort of deceitful trickery that purposely fools and victimizes those who believe. It is taking advantage of the spiritual side of life, and while it may not be a crime, it is no different than selling "fountain of youth elixirs" or creams that eradicate all wrinkles and reverse age the body. All of this is fraudulent and, when exchanged in a transaction, has fraud on its face; but when a person in authority engages in the practice, soldiers and clerics to name just two, the picture becomes more sinister, and the authority wielded causes fear in those who might usually reject such pitches. In the end, this is why the "den of robbers" designation may be more accurate than we first envisioned.

Tax Evasion

From the beginning of Jesus's life on the road to Bethlehem, His family was dealing with the Roman census—the primary aim being to keep track of those who owed tax dollars to the empire. Thus far we have witnessed the contempt the population had for tax collectors—a contempt that exists even today, especially when one is on the receiving end of an audit letter. Zaccheaus was a collector, as was Saul, then St. Matthew—both of whom reformed and adopted the way of life Jesus offered, lock, stock, and barrel. Both characters, amongst many others, are amazing stories of people being remade in the new man known as Jesus Christ.

Despite this antagonism to taxes, one will be hard pressed to find Jesus telling His followers to avoid or not pay taxes that are due. Jesus, who was not of this world or a secular kingdom, drew the line between the secular state and the Kingdom of Heaven where He resided. Even so, that line never neglected civil obligations. Jesus was always mindful that government has certain obligations, and its citizenry are obliged to support it in a host of ways—including paying taxes. When Jesus declares, "Man shall not live by bread alone, but on every word that comes from the mouth of God,"[27] He is laying a two-dimensional existence— first what is needed for day-to-day survival in the here and now and, second, the afterlife, the Kingdom where His Father resides. Jesus has offered two dimensions in His day-to-day existence, but none more compelling or important than carrying out His Father's mission in this world, to give the faithful a life in the world to come. Jesus declares:

> I am the bread of life. Whoever comes to me will never
> be hungry, and whoever believes in me will never be
> thirsty.[28]

That the Kingdom of Heaven is Jesus's raison d'etre cannot be disputed. At the same time, Jesus respects and understand the role of the temporal world and its governance. An example of this recognition, with the ultimate conclusion that the Kingdom of Heaven is in a superior position, occurs in His meeting with Pontius Pilate —the powerful Governor of Judea. The story of Pilate is one of contrasts, but what is clear is that Jesus accepts His position as Son of God yet humbles Himself in light of God the Father.

> Pilate therefore said to him, "Do you refuse to speak to me? Do you not know that I have power to release you, and power to crucify you?" Jesus answered him, "You would have no power over me unless it had been given you from above; therefore, the one who handed me over to you is guilty of a greater sin."[29]

In this fashion, Jesus acknowledges the secular authority, although He must couple secular authority with higher oversight. St. Paul understands this dual reality, in which the temporal world is located at the bottom of the continuum, better than most. His admonition is to maintain constant respect for our governing bodies. In Romans 13:1–2, the daily reality of governing institutions must be respected and adhered to.

> Let every person be subject to the governing authorities; for there is no authority except from God, and those authorities that exist have been instituted by God. Therefore, whoever resists authority resists what God has appointed, and those who resist will incur judgment.[30]

When Jesus offers to come to a Roman centurion's house, the centurion was struck by this gesture and even humbled by it. The centurion tells Jesus:

> Lord, I am not worthy to have you come under my roof; but only speak the word, and my servant will be healed. For I also am a man under authority, with

soldiers under me; and I say to one, "Go," and he goes, and to another, "Come," and he comes, and to my slave, "Do this," and the slave does it.[31]

In a sort of forlorn way, the centurion minimizes his role, almost as if he were nothing but a cog in a wheel, laboring for the empire, but implies that in Christ's Kingdom, there is something more noble and glorious. Granting this, Jesus still respects the governing body that He and every other citizen must contend with. One can discern this very readily in Mark's Gospel where Jesus taught about "giving to Caesar":

> They came and said to him, "Teacher, we know that you are truthful and are not concerned with anyone's opinion no matter what his station in life. Rather, you teach the way of God in accordance with the truth. Is it lawful or not for us to pay taxes to Caesar? Should we pay them or not?"
>
> He was aware of their hypocrisy and said to them, "Why are you trying to trap me? Bring me a denarius and let me examine it." When they brought one, he asked them, "Whose image is this, and whose inscription?" They replied and said to him, "Caesar's." Jesus said to them, "Give to Caesar what is due to Caesar, and to God what is due to God." His reply left them completely amazed at him.[32]

Jesus qualifies the paying of taxes in accordance with the published rates—no more and no less when he says: "Collect no more than the amount proscribed for you."[33]

Hence, the brilliance of Jesus Christ crosses into many spheres of influence, and the question of taxes is dealt with in justice and harmony. For, surely, you need to pay what you owe, nothing more or nothing less. For to "owe" is also a violation of His property crime analysis, in which He condemns those who do not pay back what they owe or skirt financial responsibilities. St. Paul, the former tax collector, sums this up insightfully and wraps it up in a bow of charity and love—something Jesus will always do.

> Owe no one anything, except to love one another; for the one who loves another has fulfilled the law. The commandments, "You shall not commit adultery; You shall not murder; You shall not steal; You shall not covet"; and any other commandment, are summed up in this word, "Love your neighbor as yourself." Love does no wrong to a neighbor; therefore, love is the fulfilling of the law.[34]

Conclusion

Property crime is no minor matter for Jesus Christ, for He fully discerns and understands the rotting effect of allowing these sorts of crimes to go unchecked. Property crime is largely driven by a sense of obsession that leads one to covet another's possessions. In this way, covetousness directly relates to the mental intentionality of all theft—to take illegally and to do so by direct means, or by force or threat, or deception or fraud. Jesus covers all the major property felonies, including theft and larceny, robbery and extortion, theft by deception and fraud, false statements, forgery, and utterances that cause illegal transfer and, finally, tax evasion.

Jesus expends significant energy on these offenses for a host of reasons: first, because individual rather than collective ownership advances virtue rather than vice; second, because property crimes undermine and undercut communal tranquility and the common good, and lastly, and most importantly, because the Decalogue expressly delineates property crime as direct violations of two major

Commandments: the Tenth, "Thou Shall Not Covet," and the Eighth, "Thou Shall Not Steal."

Lastly, Jesus correctly identifies situations in which position, power, or status might be used to extract, extort, or transfer property. When Jesus proclaims that the Temple has been taken over by a "den of robbers," this point is proven; for those in spiritual authority use that same authority to justify the collection of money. Similarly, Jesus accurately shows how property offenses are common in times of war and conflict.

All in all, it is an extraordinary examination that foretells modern statutory construction.

Chapter 6 Endnotes

1   See: Jay W. Richards, *Money, Greed, and God: Why Capitalism Is the Solution and Not the Problem* (HarperOne, 2010).

2   Mt 15:19–20 (NRSVCE).

3   Lk 12:33 (NRSVCE).

4   Lk 12:15 (NRSVCE).

5   Lk 19:8–9 (NIV).

6   Scott Rae and Austin Hill, T*he Virtues of Capitalism: A Moral Case for Free Markets* (Northfield Publishing, 2010).

7   See: John Paul II, encyclical *Centesimus Annus*, May 1, 1991, https://capp-usa.org/centesimus-annus/#19.

8   Leo XIII, encyclical on capital and labor *Rerum Novarum*, May 15, 1891, ¶ 15, https://capp-usa.org/rerum-novarum/#24, emphasis added.

9   Michael Barone, "Legalized Shoplifting Becomes a Racket, and Minorities Hardest Hit," *Washington Examiner,* September 6, 2023, https://www.aei.org/op-eds/legalized-shoplifting-becomes-a-racket-and-minorities-hardest-hit. See also how New York larceny is now largely nothing more than a minor misdemeanor without consequences at N.Y. Penal Law § 155.25 (2024).

10 Ex 20:17 (NRSVCE).

11 Mk 10:17–19 (NRSVCE).

12 18 Pa. Cons. Stat. § 3921 (2023).

13 18 Pa. Cons. Stat. § 3922 (2023).
14 See: Luke 18:18–20 and Mark 10:17–19.
15 18 Pa. Cons. Stat. ch. 39 (2023).
16 Mt 12:36–37 (NCB).
17 See: Lee Ohanian, "Why Shoplifting Is Now De Facto Legal In California," *Hoover Institution*, August 3, 2021, https://www.hoover.org/research/why-shoplifting-now-de-facto-legal-california.
18 Jn 10:8–10 (NRSVCE).
19 Lk 3:14 (NRSVCE).
20 See: Miriam Gebhardt and Nick Somers, *Crimes Unspoken* (Polity, 2017).
21 See Kan. Stat. Ann. Article 54 (2012).
22 Mk 11:15–19 (NRSVCE).
23 Jn 2:14–16 (NRSVCE).
24 Mt 23:27 (NRSVCE).
25 1 Cor 6:10 (NCB).
26 *Catechism of the Catholic Church*, 2nd ed. (United States Catholic Conference, 2000), § 2121.
27 Mt 4:4 (NIV).
28 Jn 6:35 (NRSVCE).
29 Jn 19:10–11 (NRSVCE).
30 Rom 13:1–2 (NRSVCE).
31 Mt 8:8–9 (NRSVCE).
32 Mk 12:14–17 (NCB).
33 Lk 3:12–13 (NRSVCE).
34 Rom 13:8–10 (NRSVCE).

Chapter 7: Christ, Crime, Moral Judgment, and Salvation

Introduction

The story of Christ's salvific mission and purpose in coming into the world is one of hope and possibility. To be sure, most criminal perpetrators languishing in American prisons generally lack all sense of hope or, at the least, the possibility for renewal and change. So often the criminal repeats the same acts over and over in a recidivist compulsion.[1] The justice system appears ill equipped to really make any meaningful difference in the lives of so many criminal actors. Most of the models for change and rehabilitation have uniformly failed. Most of the interventions suggested by the therapeutic community may make the criminal feel better but ultimately fail to trigger the type of personal change and corresponding adjustments for a happier and more productive life. Most of the psycho-social regimens are simply inadequate for meaningful reformation.[2]

Despite the system's shortcomings, the teaching of Jesus Christ offers a solid, constructive series of suggestions for not only a changed life, but a better life, rooted in the salvific power of Jesus Christ. Jesus looks to the whole person, criminal or not, sinner or saint; for every person has the potential to be in His Kingdom. Jesus opens the door to reform in ways never envisioned by the malefactor or miscreant, evildoer and agent of harm. He says so powerfully,

> What does it profit a man if he gains the whole world and loses or forfeits himself?[3]

Unfortunately, the way of life Jesus teaches has been subject to caricature and almost silly tolerance. Correcting these perceptions is one of the chief aims of this work. It is not enough to merely praise the perpetual forgiveness that Jesus appears to have no shortage of; instead it is quite another matter when one reads His demands for change, repentance, and accountability. Jesus does not equivocate in this matter and instead lays it out bluntly: Unless you repent you will all likewise perish.[4]

The plan of Jesus Christ is quite formulaic and consists of these parts:

1. Acknowledge Jesus's Purpose in Coming into the World
2. Hear and Adhere to the Teachings of Jesus Christ
3. Seek Forgiveness for Sin
4. Repent

All these steps should be analyzed when evaluating our relationship with the Son of God. It is not enough to just acknowledge Jesus's salvific aim and purpose in coming into the world.

I have come into the world as light so that everyone who believes in me may not have to remain in darkness. But if anyone listens to my words and fails to observe them, I will not pass judgment on him, for I did not come to judge the world but to save the world. Anyone who rejects me and does not accept my words already has a judge. On the last day, the word that I have spoken will serve as his judge. For I have not spoken on my own, but the Father who sent me has himself given me command about what I am to say and how I am to speak.[5]

Make no mistake about this passage—Jesus will not judge, for that is not His purpose. Instead, Jesus's presence in the world is our salvation as His Father dictates. When we read the entire quote from Jesus, He reminds us that upon our death and our last day, there will be a judge and a judgment. And what is required? He who "rejects me and does not accept my words already has a judge."[6]

More is required by Jesus than mere belief or simply listening to the substantive teachings of Christ. Change and reformation also come from hearing the Word and making a heartfelt effort to follow it. The Gospel of John summarizes this:

> Very truly, I tell you, anyone who hears my word and believes him who sent me has eternal life, and does not come under judgment, but has passed from death to life.[7]

At the third step, suggested above, the sinner must seek forgiveness and, at the fourth step, repent.

This series of actions encompasses far more than believing in a detached Jesus who doesn't hold His followers accountable or, in the alternative, to never seeing how God could issue judgments when His mercy has no measure. None of these observations accurately describes our obligations under a theory of Salvation History. Jesus makes this very plain when He observes:

> The time is fulfilled, and the kingdom of God has come near; repent, and believe in the good news.[8]

Moral Judgment and Forgiveness

One of the recurring themes in this examination has been how Jesus blends the idea of judgment with the possibility and plausibility of forgiveness. In the Christian perspective, it is not enough to make judgments for the sake of judgments. In its place, Jesus holds people to account, though never loses sight of the potential for reform, change, and a new way of human existence. Jesus never detaches His philosophy from the propriety of human conduct, remarking:

> If your brother should sin, rebuke him, and if he repents, forgive him. Even if he wrongs you seven times a day, and comes back to you seven times to say, "I am sorry," you must forgive him.[9]

See Figure 12.

Here Jesus concludes that the brother sins and at the same time declares his sorrow for the deeds he committed—and this is a judgment, but one that must be joined with the capacity to forgive. Forgiveness implies that the actor repents. And Jesus's tent of forgiveness is quite large but not without accountability.

It is, as noted, a very optimistic vision of the human agent's capacity to grow and flourish rather than experience a dark, dismal, and hopeless trek through human history. Curiously, those who love and cherish Jesus often forget this side of the Savior and falter on two fronts. First, there are those who indicate that Jesus does not judge or make moral determinations because Jesus is the fulfillment of love and charity. In that fulfillment, they believe, there is no room for those types of negative conclusions. Second, there are those who conclude that the perpetual well of forgiveness in Jesus precludes judgment.

In each case, the evaluator fails to discern His philosophy and instead misreads or misapplies the teachings of Jesus Christ. Here are a few reasons for this conclusion. Forgiveness has no real meaning unless and until one recognizes that certain behavior is an infraction, harm, or injury to another. Why would forgiveness exist unless an infraction or error was experienced or suffered? From another slant, it is clear that moral judgments, usually if not always, occur in advance of forgiveness since forgiveness is largely an intellectual operation—picking and choosing conduct which should be or can be forgiven. In short, one cannot forgive what causes no insult or injury.

As a result, Jesus ties these two elements together, namely judgment and forgiveness. In the Gospel of Luke, Jesus weaves these concepts together:

> And he said to them, "Thus it is written that the Christ would suffer and on the third day rise from the dead, and that in his name repentance and forgiveness of sins are to be proclaimed to all nations, beginning from Jerusalem."[10]

Jesus expends considerable energy explaining how forgiveness, while based in and around designated conduct worthy of our forgiveness, cannot be a restrained or stingy interaction. Forgiveness can and must be liberally applied. When Peter asks Jesus how often he should forgive, the answer signifies a generosity of spirit that most of us would have to diligently work at:

> "Lord, if my brother sins against me, how often must I forgive him? As many as seven times?" Jesus answered, "I say to you, not seven times but seventy times seven."[11]

Christ's divine capacity to forgive is incalculable. Not only must the human player forgive in charitable measure, he must also remember that the decision to forgive can never be far from the repentance. No greater story edifies this than the story of Dismas on the Cross with Jesus on Golgotha. Side by side with Jesus are two criminals who are justly suffering punishments for their deeds. One cynically says, "Are you not the Christ? Save yourself and us!"[12]

But Dismas rebukes his fellow criminal, whose life hangs in the balance, admonishing him:

> "Have you no fear of God since you are under the same sentence? In our case, we have been condemned justly, for we are getting what we deserve for our deeds. But this man has committed no wrong ... Jesus, remember me when you come into your kingdom.[13]

See Figure 13.

Crucifixion by Giovanni Battista Tiepolo, 1745–1750

As mere mortals, it is difficult to imagine Christ's capacity to forgive, yet this is precisely what Jesus demands of His followers. Jesus tells Dismas, since you have repented and sought my forgiveness, you shall inherit paradise.

> Jesus said to him, "Amen, I say to you, today you will be with me in Paradise."[14]

Repentance and Change

Another dominant theme in Christ's message holds open the possibility of reform, change, and ultimately eternal salvation. In a world saddled with crime and criminality, the message is keenly welcomed, especially amongst convicted criminals who live in often desperate settings. Our correctional system has long lost its capacity to engage in meaningful rehabilitation. Rather, the millions of prisoners housed in facilities of all sorts trudge through a bleak existence without much hope for a better day. Part of that is because the system is so secular and so dependent on the counseling modality, prisoners and criminals rarely look honestly into their own state of grace or lack thereof.[15] Given the extraordinary rates of criminal recidivism, in some circles as high as 90 percent, it is no wonder that their lives are largely left in emotional and spiritual desolation.[16]

Even as new and improved human interventions and therapeutic models come to the forefront, the data of repetitive criminality remains fairly constant. Why this is so can be explained by a host of reasons, although none is more compelling than the inability of criminal agents to admit to and take responsibility for the crimes undertaken. This dilemma becomes even more entrenched when combined with a lack of repentance. To merely ask for forgiveness is an artificial act without the aligned appraisal that my conduct is wrong, sinful, or an affront to God and man. Without this sort of moral inquisition and moral responsibility, the criminal actor simply hides in corners and between the lines and, as a result, never honestly confronts the error of his or her ways.

Because of this, the teachings of Jesus Christ regarding repentance provides the mechanism to be free and unshackled from the ravages of sin and error. Jesus directly tells His followers that if you want to be free you must submit to my teachings and those of the Father. In John, He proclaims:

> I am the resurrection and the life. Whoever believes in me, even though he dies, will live, and everyone who lives and believes in me will never die. Do you believe this?[17]

Hence, it is not enough to just be repentant or sorry for one's wrongdoing. Nor is it enough to repeatedly ask for forgiveness without external action. When forgiveness is joined to repentance, one other criterion emerges, namely "change." If one fails to change or alter his or her life, the other variables of forgiveness and repentance remain hollow. Jesus calls upon His followers to take the harder road and to assume that living in accordance with His teachings is often a tough sell. Take up your Cross, Jesus states in the Gospel of Mark.

> Anyone who wishes to follow me must deny himself, take up his cross, and follow me. For whoever wishes to save his life will lose it, but whoever loses his life for my sake and the sake of the gospel will save it. What does it profit a man to gain the whole world and forfeit his very life?[18]

Change is a mandate for the Christian hoping to be faithful to the teachings of Jesus Christ, and this requirement is equally true for both the criminal and the virtuous citizen. To believe means more than arriving at a mere philosophical conclusion regarding

Jesus; rather, it is an affirmative decision to adopt the Christian life, which must be also chosen. This is no easy road, but it is a path to change that rests comfortably with the wisdom of Jesus.

> Only live in a manner worthy of the gospel of Christ. Then, whether I come and see you or simply hear news of you from a distance, I will know that you are standing firm and united in spirit, striving together for the faith of the gospel.[19]

In sum, it is not enough to plead for forgiveness and then repent without the added proviso that one change from a sinner to a saintlier person. For Jesus reminds His followers that they need to accept His teachings and live in accordance thereto, because a failure to change will result in His Father issuing judgment. Jesus confirms this in Gospel of John:

> But if anyone listens to my words and fails to observe them, I will not pass judgment on him, for I did not come to judge the world but to save the world. Anyone who rejects me and does not accept my words already has a judge. On the last day, the word that I have spoken will serve as his judge.[20]

Only when the follower of Jesus blends the acts of forgiveness, repentance, and change can true reform ever take place. All else can only be described as aspirational. In integrating Jesus into our day-to-day existence, we truly can and do change in accordance with His perfection. No better example posed in the New Testament edifies this hopeful path to restoration and health more than the adulteress in the Temple. All three elements appear clearly in the story. First, the woman looks to Jesus during the impending stoning and He intervenes. Those ready to cast those stones are essentially stared down or made shameful by Jesus. To further buttress their shame, the stoning crowd runs off. Jesus then remarks to the woman::

"Woman, where are they? Has no one condemned you?" She replied, "No one, sir." "Neither do I condemn you," Jesus said. "Go on your way, and sin no more."[21]

See Figure 14.

To sin no more is the affirmative obligation, the change that Jesus requires. Until and when that happens the question of repentance and forgiveness has yet to be resolved. Only the change, abandoning sin, guarantees compliance with the Way, the Truth, and the Life.

Chapter 7 Endnotes

1 "Recidivism and Reentry," Bureau of Justice Statistics, accessed October 12, 2024, https://bjs.ojp.gov/topics/recidivism-and-reentry.
2 Because of this many argue for the elimination or radical reformation of prisons. See: Jeffery Shockley, "Why Prisons Fail to Rehabilitate People," *Prison Journalism Project*, June 22, 2023, https://prisonjournalismproject.org/2023/06/22/why-prisons-fail-to-rehabilitate-people.
3 Lk 9:25 (NCB).
4 Lk 13:3 (RSVCE).
5 Jn 12:46–49 (NCB).
6 Jn 12:48 (NCB).
7 Jn 5:24 (NRSVACE).
8 Mk 1:15 (NRSVACE).
9 Lk 17:3–4 (NCB).
10 Lk 24:46–47 (NCB).
11 Mt 18:21–22 (NCB).
12 Lk 23:39 (NCB).
13 Lk 23:40–43 (NCB).
14 Lk 23:43 (NCB).
15 See: Sung Joon Jang and Byron R. Johnson, "Religion and Rehabilitation as Moral Reform: Conceptualization and Preliminary Evidence," *American Journal of Criminal Justice* 14 (2022): 1–27, https://doi.org/10.1007/s12103-022-09707-3.
16 Tenzing Lahdon, "From the Desk of BJA," in *Justice Matters Newsletter*, November 2023, https://bja.ojp.gov/news/justice-matters/desk-bja-november-2023.
17 Jn 11:25–26 (NCB).
18 Mk 8:34–36 (NCB).
19 Phil 1:27 (NCB).

20 Jn 12:46–48 (NCB).
21 Jn 8:10–11 (NCB).